PHONICS for Reading

THIRD LEVEL

Cover Design: Pat Lucas
Illustrators: Laurel Aiello
　　　　　　　Leslie Alfred McGrath

Anita Archer
James Flood
Diane Lapp
Linda Lungren

CURRICULUM ASSOCIATES®, INC.

ISBN 978-0-89187-993-0

©2009, 2002, 1993—Curriculum Associates, Inc.
North Billerica, MA 01862

No part of this book may be reproduced by any means
without written permission from the publisher.

All Rights Reserved. Printed in USA.

15 14 13 12 11 10 9 8 7 6 5 4 3

Table of Contents

Lesson	Page	Lesson	Page
Lesson 1	4	Lesson 20	80
Lesson 2	8	Lesson 21	84
Lesson 3	12	Lesson 22	88
Lesson 4	16	Lesson 23	92
Lesson 5	20	Lesson 24	96
Lesson 6	24	Lesson 25	100
Lesson 7	28	Lesson 26	104
Lesson 8	32	Lesson 27	108
Lesson 9	36	Lesson 28	112
Lesson 10	40	Lesson 29	116
Lesson 11	44	Lesson 30	120
Lesson 12	48	Lesson 31	124
Lesson 13	52	Lesson 32	128
Lesson 14	56	Lesson 33	132
Lesson 15	60	Lesson 34	136
Lesson 16	64	Lesson 35	140
Lesson 17	68	Lesson 36	144
Lesson 18	72	Word Lists	148
Lesson 19	76		

LESSON 1

■ **New Sound.** Say the word.

m<u>oo</u>n

A. **New Words.** Say each sound. Say each word.

1. f<u>oo</u>d   s<u>oo</u>n   f<u>ee</u>d
2. fl<u>ir</u>t   br<u>oo</u>m   fl<u>ow</u>
3. sp<u>oo</u>n   br<u>ai</u>n   sm<u>oo</u>th
4. ch<u>oo</u>se   sp<u>or</u>t   t<u>oo</u>th
5. Soon we shall be home.
6. I need to get a broom.
7. Jill likes to eat with her spoon.
8. It is hard to choose the winner.

B. **Challenge Words.** Say the words.

rooster (1 2)   scooter (1 2)   moonlight (1 2)   cartoon (1 2)   toothbrush (1 2)

schoolroom (1 2)   teaspoon (1 2)   shampoo (1 2)   raccoon (1 2)   afternoon (1 2 3)

C. **Word Parts.** Say the words.

<u>un</u>lock   <u>dis</u>trust   agree<u>able</u>   hand<u>ful</u>

D. **Words with Word Parts.** Say the words.

1. <u>un</u>real   <u>dis</u>card   <u>dis</u>may   <u>un</u>chain
2. help<u>ful</u>   teach<u>able</u>   drink<u>able</u>   faith<u>ful</u>
3. <u>un</u>think<u>able</u>   <u>dis</u>gust<u>ing</u>   <u>dis</u>trust<u>ful</u>   <u>un</u>grate<u>ful</u>

E. **Sight Words.** Say the words.

all	call	hall	ball	tall
because	through	also	about	
care	find	were	one	your
who	some	how	many	

F. **Passages.** Read each part of the story. Write the story part number under the picture that goes with each story part.

Tooth Care

Part 1

When you were born, you did not have teeth. The food you ate had to be soft because you did not have teeth. You ate soft food with a spoon. After a while, one tooth came through your gums. That may have hurt a bit. Soon after that, more and more teeth came through your gums. A grown-up has thirty-two (32) teeth. Some are big and some are not. They are all hard, white, and smooth.

Because your teeth are important to you, you must take care of them. You need your teeth to eat your food. Teeth are also part of a big smile. It is not hard to take care of your teeth; it just takes time.

Part 2

It is very important to keep your teeth clean. The food you eat can stick to your teeth. If the food stays there, it will hurt the tooth. The best way to clean your teeth is to brush them with a toothbrush. A toothbrush cleans your teeth as a broom cleans the pavement. You should brush your teeth up and down to get all of the hidden food bits. Brush your teeth when you get up in the morning and when you go to bed each night. You should also brush your teeth after each meal. Brushing your teeth is the best way for you to care for your teeth.

Part 3

A dentist helps you take care of your teeth. A dentist cleans your teeth and shows you the best way to brush them. Your dentist tells you the best toothbrush to get. Dentists also help if you have pain in your gums or teeth. The pain tells you to go see your dentist. It may mean you are not taking care of your teeth right.

If food stays on a tooth, it can make a hole in the tooth. A hole in the tooth hurts. Your dentist will find the hole and fill it. This will make the pain stop.

If you do not like pain, brush your teeth after each meal. You should see your dentist for checkups, too. If you take care of your teeth, they will serve you well.

G. **Practice Activity 1.** Read each question. Look back at the story on page 5. Fill in each blank with the best word.

Part 1

1. **WHY** do we have to eat soft food when we are little?

    We have to eat soft food because we have no _____.

2. **HOW** many teeth do grown-ups have?

    Grown-ups have _____ teeth.

3. **WHY** are teeth important?

    Teeth help us eat _____.

Part 2

4. **WHAT** is the best way to clean your teeth?

    The best way to clean your teeth is to _____ them with a _____.

5. **WHEN** should you brush your teeth?

    You should brush your teeth when you get up in the morning and before you go to _____. You should also brush your teeth after each _____.

Part 3

6. **WHO** can clean your teeth and show you how to brush them?

    A _____ can clean your teeth and show you how to brush them.

7. **WHAT** might happen if food stays on a tooth?

    The food might make a _____ in the tooth.

8. **HOW** can you take care of your teeth?

    You can _____ your teeth and see your dentist for _____.

☐ Correct

H. Practice Activity 2. Underline all the endings that make sense.

1. A girl can _____.
   a. sit in a schoolroom
   b. stir tea with a teaspoon
   c. clean her teeth with a toothbrush
   d. shampoo a horse in a sink

2. Fred can _____.
   a. sweep moonlight with a broom
   b. ride a scooter to the store
   c. see moonlight during the afternoon
   d. feed peanuts to a cartoon

☐ Correct

I. Practice Activity 3. Fill in each blank with the best word.

| handful | unlock | drinkable | helpful | dismay | agreeable |
| unreal | discard | grateful | teachable | unchain | distrustful |

1. Please _____ the car so we can get in.
2. Janis fed a _____ of peanuts to the raccoon.
3. Tom fixed the broken lock and painted the gate. Tom was very _____.
4. The water was clean. It was _____.
5. The day was like a dream. It seemed _____ to Janis.
6. If you throw something away, you _____ it.
7. Barb was very _____ for the help we gave her.
8. If you can teach a dog a trick, the dog is _____.
9. You should be _____ of someone who steals.
10. Pete groaned with _____ as he missed the ball.
11. Joan would be more _____ if she would smile sometimes.
12. _____ the dog's leash from the gate, please.

☐ Correct

LESSON 2

A. New Words. Say each sound. Say each word.

1. m<u>oo</u>n   c<u>oo</u>l   sh<u>ow</u>
2. n<u>oo</u>n   sh<u>ee</u>t   t<u>oo</u>l
3. sh<u>oo</u>t   m<u>oo</u>se   b<u>oa</u>st
4. b<u>oo</u>st   m<u>oa</u>n   sn<u>oo</u>ze
5. Rover likes to bark at the moon.
6. What is the noon meeting about?
7. The moose roamed through the forest.
8. Dad will take a snooze before dinner.

B. Challenge Words. Say the words.

har·poon   moon·beam   whirl·pool   noon·time   mon·soon
 1 2   1 2   1 2   1 2   1 2

home·room   class·room   plain·tiff   har·bor   in·crease
 1 2   1 2   1 2   1 2   1 2

C. Word Parts. Say the words.

<u>un</u>lock   <u>dis</u>trust   agree<u>able</u>   hand<u>ful</u>

D. Words with Word Parts. Say the words.

1. <u>dis</u>play   <u>un</u>snap   <u>un</u>rest   <u>dis</u>turb
2. fix<u>able</u>   pain<u>ful</u>   reach<u>able</u>   faith<u>ful</u>
3. <u>dis</u>taste<u>ful</u>   <u>un</u>mend<u>able</u>   <u>un</u>sink<u>able</u>   <u>un</u>skill<u>ful</u>

E. Sight Words. Say the words.

all	tall	ball	fall	call
because	also	through	about	find
where	your	now	how	why

F. Passages. Read each part of the story. Write the story part number under the picture that goes with each story part.

Chuck and His Teeth

Part 1

It was nine and time for Chuck to go to bed. He got into bed and felt the cool sheets.
20 He lay in bed, but he could not sleep because the moon was too bright. He got up and
39 shut the drapes. Then he got back into his bed and went to sleep.
53 "Rats!" Tom Tooth said to his sister. "I was hoping he got up to clean us. That beef he
72 had for dinner is still stuck on my back."
81 "Part of this morning's bran muffin is right next to me, too," said Nan Tooth. "This is all
99 very distasteful. I hate to say it, but it may be time for some pain. Chuck needs a boost."

Part 2

118 About noon the next day, Chuck sat down to eat lunch. He felt a bit of pain in his
137 tooth, but the pain was not bad. Then he had a drink of milk. "My tooth hurts!" he said
156 with a moan. "Mom! My tooth hurts a lot. Can you make it stop?"
170 "I can't make it stop hurting, Chuck. We will have to go to the dentist. She will check
188 your teeth and make the pain stop. I will check with the nurse to see when we can go."
207 Mom left the room and came back after three or four minutes. "The dentist can see you
224 at three. For now, stay still and rest."

Part 3

232 "Well, Chuck, that tooth will be fine soon," said the dentist. "I can also see that you
249 need to brush your teeth more. I will clean your teeth and show you how to take care
267 of your teeth at home. Your toothbrush is an important tool, but you must use it more
284 than you have been. Let me show you," she said as she started to clean Chuck's teeth.
301 "I feel so clean and fresh!" Nan Tooth said. "It's a shame we had to do it that way,
320 Tom. I feel bad about it."
326 "Chuck is smart, Nan," said Tom Tooth. "I think he will brush us more now. He needs
343 us as much as we need him. I bet we will have a clean and neat home from this day on!"
364

G. **Practice Activity 1.** Read each question. Look back at the story on page 9. Fill in each blank with the best word.

Part 1

1. **WHY** did Chuck get up?

   Chuck got up to shut the _____.

2. **WHAT** did Tom Tooth hope that Chuck would do?

   Tom Tooth hoped that Chuck would _____ his teeth.

3. **WHAT** did Nan Tooth say that Chuck needed?

   Nan Tooth said that it might be time for some _____.

Part 2

4. **WHAT** did Chuck tell his mom?

   Chuck said, "My tooth _____!"

5. **WHERE** did Chuck have to go?

   Chuck had to go to the _____.

Part 3

6. **WHAT** did the dentist tell Chuck?

   The dentist said, "You need to _____ your teeth more."

7. **WHAT** did the dentist do?

   The dentist _____ Chuck's teeth.

8. **HOW** did Nan Tooth and Tom Tooth feel?

   They felt fresh and _____.

☐ Correct

H. Practice Activity 2. Fill in each blank with the best word.

| noontime | toothbrush | classroom | scooter |
| shampoo | raccoon | moonlight | rooster |

1. Tom rode the _____ down the road.
2. Dennis put the _____ in the bathtub.
3. After lunch, the children went back to the _____.
4. In the bright _____, we could see the raccoons.
5. We saw the _____ run inside the log.
6. The red _____ wakes us up in the morning.
7. At the store, Janis got a green _____ for her teeth.
8. Trish will wash the car at _____.

☐ Correct

I. Practice Activity 3. Fill in each blank with the best word.

1. Janis will _____ her jacket.
      unsnap   unreal   unchain
2. Barb and Fred are making a raft. Barb has a _____ of nails.
      painful   handful   helpful
3. The lock broke, but I think it is _____.
      fixable   teachable   drinkable
4. I don't like games. I _____ them very much.
      discard   dislike   display
5. Dad is taking a nap. Do not _____ him.
      disturb   dislike   distrust
6. The box is on the top shelf, but I think it is _____.
      fixable   teachable   reachable

☐ Correct

LESSON 3

A. **New Words.** Say each sound. Say each word.

1. r<u>oo</u>m   l<u>oo</u>se   st<u>oo</u>l
2. r<u>oo</u>t   st<u>ea</u>l   r<u>oo</u>f
3. b<u>oo</u>th   m<u>oo</u>d   b<u>ea</u>ch
4. h<u>oo</u>p   l<u>ea</u>se   bl<u>oo</u>m
5. My little gray cat likes to sit on that stool.
6. Her tennis ball is stuck on the roof of your shed.
7. Ken's mood will be better after he gets some rest.
8. Who is the best person to enter the hoop contest?

B. **Challenge Words.** Say the words.

dustproof (1 2)   booster (1 2)   loosen (1 2)   baboon (1 2)   tattoo (1 2)

foolproof (1 2)   mushroom (1 2)   drainpipe (1 2)   president (1 2 3)   innkeeper (1 2 3)

C. **Word Parts.** Say the words.

<u>un</u>lock   <u>dis</u>trust   agree<u>able</u>   hand<u>ful</u>

D. **Words with Word Parts.** Say the words.

1. <u>dis</u>own   <u>un</u>load   <u>un</u>leash   <u>dis</u>please
2. afford<u>able</u>   boast<u>ful</u>   need<u>ful</u>   harm<u>ful</u>
3. <u>disagreeable</u>   <u>unfaithful</u>   <u>distressing</u>   <u>unhelpful</u>

E. **Sight Words.** Say the words.

all	fall	call	hall	tall
about	because	want	through	also
put	now	one	find	been

F. **Passages.** Read each part of the story. Write the story part number under the picture that goes with each story part.

Room to Grow

Part 1

19 "No, Carl, you may not go until you clean your room. Look at it! I bet a baboon would
40 turn up his nose at it! I have been telling you for three days to clean it. If you start soon,
55 you could get to the beach by about noon." Then his mom left the room.
75 "This put me in a bad mood!" Carl said to his dog, Tattoo. "I want all of this stuff. There
95 is just too much for this room. Do you see that hoop? Coach Green gave it to me. I can't
118 part with it. I like that big stool, too. I got it cheap at a yard sale last week. I might use it
    someday." Carl sat on the bed. "I need to think about this," he said to Tattoo.

Part 2

134 After a while, Carl got up. He started to pick things up. He made his bed. Then he slid
153 the hoop from Coach Green under the bed. "It fits, Tattoo," he said. "I wish the stool
170 were flat so I could slide it under the bed." Carl stopped and said, "My room is cleaner,
188 but I am still not through."
194 Carl dusted his desk and then swept with a broom. There was a lot of dust. Soon the
212 room started to look clean. "Well, Tattoo," Carl said, "what shall I do with that stool? It
229 may have been a steal, but it may have to go." Tattoo just gave Carl a glum look.
247 "Wait!" Carl yelled. "I have it!"

Part 3

253 Carl left his room and went down to the yard. When he came back, he had three pots
272 with plants in them. He put the stool in the corner by his window. He put one plant on
291 top of the stool and the rest on the steps.
301 "Mom," Carl yelled, "now my room is clean. Come and see it." Mom came in and
317 smiled. Carl's room was neat and clean. Then she saw the stool in the corner.
332 "It's more than a stool, Mom," Carl said. It is also a plant stand. Those plants need
349 light to grow. Look at this rose. It's about to bloom. I got the whole root when I dug it
369 up. Now may I go to the beach?"
377

G. **Practice Activity 1.** Read each question. Look back at the story on page 13. Fill in each blank with the best word.

Part 1

1. **WHAT** did Carl have to do?

    Carl had to _____ his room.

2. **WHO** gave Carl a hoop?

    _____ _____ gave Carl a hoop.

3. **WHERE** did Carl get the big stool?

    Carl got the stool at a _____ _____.

Part 2

4. **WHERE** did Carl put the hoop?

    Carl put the hoop under the _____.

5. **WHAT** did Carl think he might have to get rid of?

    Carl felt he might have to get rid of the _____.

Part 3

6. **WHAT** did Carl get from the yard?

    Carl got _____ _____ with plants in them.

7. **WHERE** did he put the plants?

    He put the plants on top of the stool and on its _____.

8. **WHAT** was the stool now?

    The stool was a _____ _____.

☐ Correct

H. Practice Activity 2. Underline all the endings that make sense.

1. The children can _____ .
   a. ride on a moonbeam
   b. see a baboon at the zoo
   c. vote for a homeroom president
   d. shampoo a big baboon in the sink

2. After lunch, the art teacher will _____.
   a. go back to the classroom
   b. loosen the lids on the jars of paint
   c. sweep the moonlight into a box
   d. make a cartoon with a crayon

☐ Correct

I. Practice Activity 3. Fill in each blank with the best word.

1. Dad will _____ the fishing rods from the car.
       unchain   unreal   unload

2. Please do not _____ the children who are napping.
       displease   disturb   discard

3. Jeff ate a _____ of food.
       harmful   spoonful   helpful

4. Ann can fix the broken stool. The stool is _____.
       agreeable   fixable   teachable

5. Mr. Smith will _____ the classroom in the school.
       unsnap   unrest   unlock

6. Jane gave Bart a _____ of peanuts.
       skillful   painful   handful

7. Not all bugs are _____ to a garden.
       spoonful   handful   harmful

8. The cups on the top shelf are _____.
       teachable   reachable   agreeable

☐ Correct   ☐ Checking up

LESSON 4

■ **New Sound.** Say the words.

s<u>aw</u>   f<u>au</u>lt

A. New Words. Say each sound. Say each word.

1. y<u>aw</u>n   f<u>au</u>lt   cl<u>aw</u>
2. h<u>au</u>l   fl<u>oa</u>t   dr<u>aw</u>
3. sp<u>oo</u>l   cr<u>aw</u>l   c<u>oo</u>l
4. l<u>aw</u>n   l<u>oa</u>n   c<u>au</u>se
5. The cat's claw is sharp.
6. The truck will haul this load away.
7. They had to crawl through the cave.
8. Look at how green the lawn is!

B. Challenge Words. Say the words.

ex̆haust   author   auburn   August   drawing
 1 2   1 2   1 2   1 2   1 2

lawn mower   lawyer   igloo   imperfect   advertise
 1   2   3   1 2   1 2   1 2 3   1 2 3

C. Word Parts. Say the words.

<u>re</u>turn   <u>pre</u>heat   mad<u>ness</u>   help<u>less</u>

D. Words with Word Parts. Say the words.

1. <u>re</u>fill   <u>un</u>seen   <u>pre</u>pay   <u>dis</u>card
2. end<u>less</u>   fresh<u>ness</u>   port<u>able</u>   grate<u>ful</u>
3. <u>re</u>turn<u>able</u> <u>re</u>pay<u>able</u> <u>un</u>think<u>able</u> boast<u>fulness</u>
4. <u>un</u>prevent<u>able</u> <u>dis</u>trust<u>fulness</u>

E. Sight Words. Say the words.

other   another   mother   brother
many   also   call   find   about
been   come   people   there   were

F. **Passages.** Read each part of the story. Write the story part number under the picture that goes with each story part.

Apollo 11 to the Moon

Part 1

People have been thinking about the moon for a long time. On a bright night, many people look at the moon. Some people dream about the moon or make wishes on the moon. Others see a man on the moon. Still others say the moon is made of cheese!

We get more and more facts about the moon each year. The moon has no light of its own. The light we see comes from the sun, which is 400 times bigger than the moon. There is also no wind on the moon.

Part 2

In 1969, three men went to the moon in a rocket called *Apollo 11*. *Apollo 11* needed help to get to the moon. Some of the help came from a *Saturn* rocket. Its one job was to help *Apollo 11* and the three men reach the moon. The *Saturn* rocket helped launch *Apollo 11*.

A big tractor called a "crawler" hauled *Apollo 11* and the *Saturn* rocket to the launch pad. Soon they blasted off. After a short while, a part of the *Saturn* rocket came off. That part of the *Saturn* rocket did not go to the moon with *Apollo 11*. This was the first step in the plan to get *Apollo 11* to the moon. Then another part of the *Saturn* rocket blasted off and sent *Apollo 11* speeding to the moon. *Apollo 11* had to get close to the moon and into the moon's orbit.

Part 3

When the men got close to the moon, part of *Apollo 11* stayed in orbit. The other part, with two men inside, landed on the moon. The men had many jobs to do, such as finding some rocks to take home and taking many snapshots of the moon. When they lifted off from the moon, they needed to lighten their load. They had to leave some things on the moon, such as their backpacks and boots. Then they returned to the other part of *Apollo 11* still in orbit.

Apollo 11 left the moon's orbit and started the long trip home. The trip home was much like the trip to the moon. All went well on the return trip, and *Apollo 11* splashed down in the water as planned.

In 1969, three men went to the moon and returned. It was a trip they would not soon forget.

G. **Practice Activity 1.** Read each question. Look back at the story on page 17. Fill in each blank with the best word or number.

Part 1

1. **HOW** long have people been thinking about the moon?

   People have been thinking about the moon for a _____ _____.

2. **WHERE** is the light coming from that we see on the moon?

   The light we see on the moon is coming from the _____.

3. **HOW** much bigger is the sun than the moon?

   The sun is _____ times bigger than the moon.

Part 2

4. **WHAT** did the *Saturn* rocket do?

   The *Saturn* rocket helped to _____ Apollo 11.

5. **WHAT** helped *Apollo 11* reach the launch pad?

   A big tractor called a "_____" helped *Apollo 11* reach the launch pad.

Part 3

6. **WHAT** did the other part of *Apollo 11* do while one part landed on the moon?

   The other part of the *Apollo 11* craft stayed in _____.

7. **WHAT** did the men on the moon have to find?

   The men had to find _____.

8. **WHERE** did *Apollo 11* land on the return trip?

   Apollo 11 _____ down in the water on the return trip.

☐ Correct

H. **Practice Activity 2.** Fill in each blank with the best word.

| August | author | exhaust | president |
| advertise | classroom | lawyer | moonlight |

1. Mr. Martin will _____ the sale in this week's paper.
2. Some of the hottest days are in _____.
3. They voted for a _____ to run the club.
4. It was a dark night because there was very little _____.
5. After school, the teacher worked in his _____.
6. Black smoke came from the truck's _____ pipe.
7. Who is the _____ of this children's story?
8. He needs a _____ to help him win his rights.

☐ Correct

I. **Practice Activity 3.** Fill in each blank with the best word.

1. On Thursday, Fred will pay for the next three weeks of rent.

   Fred will _____ the rent.

   preheat
   prevent
   prepay

2. Jeff will fill the cups for the third time.

   Jeff will _____ the cups with coffee.

   return
   refill
   rerun

3. The buns were just baked.

   You will like the _____ of the buns.

   madness
   coolness
   freshness

4. Jill thanked us for helping her.

   She was very _____.

   grateful
   spoonful
   handful

5. The road went on and on.

   The road seemed _____.

   helpless
   endless
   nameless

6. You can take the TV from room to room.

   The TV is _____.

   portable
   reachable
   drinkable

☐ Correct

19

LESSON 5

A. **New Words.** Say each sound. Say each word.

1. fr<u>au</u>d   str<u>aw</u>   st<u>oo</u>l
2. dr<u>ea</u>m   dr<u>aw</u>n   v<u>au</u>lt
3. h<u>aw</u>k   fr<u>ee</u>d   sh<u>aw</u>l
4. fl<u>ow</u>   fl<u>aw</u>   fl<u>ee</u>
5. Our cow, Bessy, eats straw.
6. Is the vault made out of steel or copper?
7. Lin gave her mother a red silk shawl.
8. The painter corrected a flaw in his work.

B. **Challenge Words.** Say the words.

applause (1 2)   coleslaw (1 2)   withdrawn (1 2)   sawdust (1 2)   drawback (1 2)

autumn (1 2)   sweepstakes (1 2)   wayside (1 2)   bridegroom (1 2)   entertainment (1 2 3 4)

C. **Word Parts.** Say the words.

<u>re</u>turn   <u>pre</u>heat   mad<u>ness</u>   help<u>less</u>

D. **Words with Word Parts.** Say the words.

1. <u>pre</u>tend   <u>re</u>port   <u>dis</u>may   <u>un</u>hurt
2. name<u>less</u>   like<u>ness</u>   afford<u>able</u>   pocket<u>ful</u>
3. <u>re</u>mark<u>able</u>   <u>dis</u>tinct<u>ness</u>   <u>un</u>teach<u>able</u>   <u>un</u>thank<u>ful</u><u>ness</u>

E. **Sight Words.** Say the words.

other	another	brother	mother	
many	also	animals	because	want
there	what	were	now	call

F. **Passages.** Read each part of the story. Write the story part number under the picture that goes with each story part.

The Art Show

Part 1

"What a way to spend the afternoon!" Paul said to his brother Fred. "I want to go to the beach, but I have to go to the art show in the park. My art teacher said that we all have to go to this show. Next week each of us has to report to the class. It's part of the grade for the class," Paul moaned. "At least you said you would go with me, Fred. That will make it less painful. Let's get our bikes and go now."

"Be a good sport, Paul," said Fred. "Many of the kids from your class will be at the art show. It may turn into a fun afternoon. OK, let's go."

Part 2

Paul and Fred rode down the street to the park. When they got to the lawn on the east side of the park, they saw hundreds of people. Some were selling things but many others were just looking. Paul and Fred put the bikes in a bike rack and locked them. Then they went to see what the artists had drawn.

"Look at this!" Paul said. "It's just a straw stuck to the side of a box. Is this art? It has a name, too. It's called "Straw Dream." You can own it for $45. Who would pay $45 for this? I hope this work of art is not a fraud. Let's go to the other end of this row."

On the way, they stopped to look at a portrait of a man with a hawk on his hand. "He looks sad," Fred said. "He also looks like he is speaking to that hawk. Do you think the hawk's claws are hurting the man?" he asked.

Part 3

Soon they came to a booth where a man on a stool was drawing portraits in ink. Paul and Fred stopped to look. The artist worked very fast, and his drawings were flawless. "What a remarkable likeness for such fast work!" Paul said in surprise. "Some of this art is art after all!"

"There is a band playing on the lawn," Fred said. "We can go there for some entertainment if you like."

"Who needs a band for entertainment?" Paul said with a grin. "When I saw Jill, she said we had to go see a painting down this way. She said the painting is called "Artist's Flaw." It's just a big white blank with a black border. I could do art like that! Let's go see it."

G. **Practice Activity 1.** Read each question. Look back at the story on page 21. Fill in each blank with the best word or number.

Part 1

1. **WHERE** did Paul have to go?

   He had to go to an _____ _____ in the park.

2. **WHY** did Paul have to go?

   Paul had to go to the art show because his _____

   _____ said that his class had to go.

3. **WHO** said that he would go to the art show with Paul?

   Paul's brother _____ said that he would go to the art show with Paul.

Part 2

4. **WHAT** were people doing at the art show?

   Some people were _____ things, but many others were just

   _____.

5. **HOW** much did "Straw Dream" cost?

   "Straw Dream" cost _____.

6. **WHAT** did the man in the portrait have on his hand?

   He had a _____ on his hand.

Part 3

7. **WHAT** was the man in the booth doing?

   The man was _____ portraits in ink.

8. **WHAT** painting did Paul and Fred go to see?

   Paul and Fred went to see a painting called "_____

   _____."

☐ Correct

H. **Practice Activity 2.** Fill in each blank with the best word.

coleslaw   **sweepstakes**   **bridegroom**   **applause**
entertainment   **autumn**   **drainpipe**   **sawdust**

1. Next to the lumber mill were piles of _____.
2. The bride and the _____ left after the wedding.
3. There was much _____ when the play ended.
4. We ate _____ at the picnic.
5. The ring fell down the sink's _____.
6. The season after summer is _____.
7. Do you think you could ever win the _____?
8. For your _____, I would like to sing a song.

☐ Correct

I. **Practice Activity 3.** Fill in each blank with the best word.

1. Mom will heat up the food left from last night's dinner.
   Mom will _____ the food.
       reheat
       report
       return

2. The drawing looks just like Janis.
   The drawing is a perfect _____ of Janis.
       freshness
       madness
       likeness

3. The doctor helps keep people well.
   The doctor hopes to _____ illness.
       preheat
       pretend
       prevent

4. If you cannot get into a room, you may need
   to _____ the door.
       unhurt
       unlock
       unseen

5. The work at the store never seemed to stop.
   The work seemed _____.
       nameless
       helpless
       endless

6. Mr. Martin will take the TV back to the store.
   He will _____ the TV to the store.
       refill
       return
       reheat

☐ Correct

LESSON 6

A. **New Words.** Say each sound. Say each word.

1. l<u>aw</u> ch<u>oo</u>se p<u>au</u>se
2. l<u>aw</u>n th<u>aw</u> spr<u>aw</u>l
3. spr<u>ai</u>n j<u>aw</u> j<u>ar</u>
4. p<u>aw</u> thr<u>ow</u> l<u>au</u>nch
5. Jane plans to study law next fall.
6. I hope the food does not thaw on the way to the picnic!
7. Did you see the size of that gorilla's jaw?
8. Will they launch this rocket at noon or at three o'clock?

B. **Challenge Words.** Say the words.

pauper (1 2)   sawmill (1 2)   because (1 2)   seesaw (1 2)   awesome (1 2)

launder (1 2)   autoharp (1 2 3)   automatic (1 2 3 4)   misinterpret (1 2 3 4)   understood (1 2 3)

C. **Word Parts.** Say the words.

<u>re</u>turn   <u>pre</u>heat   mad<u>ness</u>   help<u>less</u>

D. **Words with Word Parts.** Say the words.

1. <u>re</u>choose   <u>pre</u>dict   <u>un</u>pack   <u>dis</u>gust
2. speech<u>less</u>   smooth<u>ness</u>   bucket<u>ful</u>   do<u>able</u>
3. <u>re</u>cord<u>er</u>   <u>pre</u>vent<u>able</u>   <u>pre</u>sent<u>able</u>   <u>re</u>fill<u>able</u>

E. **Sight Words.** Say the words.

other   another   mother   brother

many   through   also   one   want

about   would   how   from   now

F. **Passages.** Read each part of the story. Write the story part number under the picture that goes with each story part.

A Painful Lesson

Part 1

"We all miss you at school," Jan said to Trish. "I hope you got the card we sent. Miss Parks let me choose the card because I said I would see you today." Trish smiled but did not speak.

"This seems very odd," Jan said. "This is the first time I have seen you speechless. Is your jaw still painful?" Jan stopped and then said in disgust, "I keep doing that! You can't speak with that hurt jaw, yet I keep asking you about things! Let's play cards for a while. Tell me when you need to take a rest."

They played a card game. After a while, Jan left and said she would be back soon.

Part 2

"Did you see Trish this afternoon?" Jan's mother asked when Jan got home. "I understand she will have to rest for a long time."

"Yes, I saw her," Jan said. "We played cards for a while, but I left because she seemed to be in pain. She has a broken jaw and three cracked ribs. Her left arm is also sprained. That car crash caused a mess for Trish. She will miss a lot of school, too. Miss Parks is taping some of the school lessons. Trish can play the tapes on her tape recorder, but it's not the same as being in school with the rest of us. It must be hard staying in bed all day," Jan said with a sigh.

Part 3

"It's a shame," Jan's mother said. "It's also too bad because her pain could have been prevented. Trish's mother said Trish did not have her seat belt on. Think about it. Seat belts can save lives. In fact, many people think we should have a seat belt law. I hope you and your pals will not soon forget this lesson."

  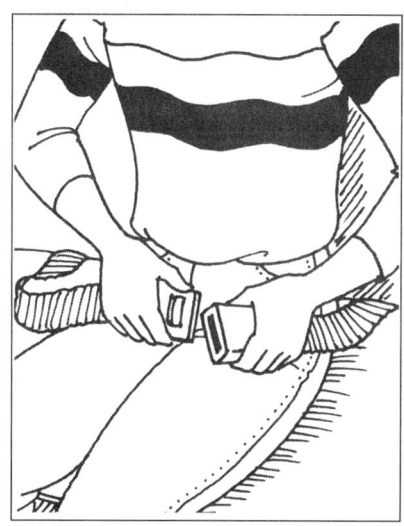

G. Practice Activity 1. Read each question. Look back at the story on page 25. Fill in each blank with the best word.

Part 1

1. **WHY** didn't Trish speak?

   Trish didn't speak because she hurt her _____.

2. **WHO** came to see Trish?

   _____ came to see Trish.

3. **WHAT** did Trish and Jan do?

   They played _____.

Part 2

4. **HOW** did Trish get hurt?

   Trish was in a _____ _____.

5. **WHAT** must Trish do?

   Trish must stay in _____ all day.

6. **HOW** is Miss Parks helping Trish?

   Miss Parks is _____ some of the school lessons.

Part 3

7. **WHY** did Trish get hurt?

   Trish did not have her _____ _____ on.

8. **WHAT** can seat belts do?

   Seat belts can save _____.

☐ Correct

H. **Practice Activity 2.** Fill in each blank with the best word.

straw	yawn	haul	launch
hawk	drawn	fault	pause

1. They hope to _____ the rocket on Thursday afternoon.
2. Janis drank the smooth milk with a _____.
3. Dennis will _____ the junk away in his jeep.
4. Jim's car ran off the highway during the storm. It was not Jim's _____.
5. Peg has _____ three portraits in art class.
6. When Ted woke up from his nap, I saw him _____.
7. I saw a big bird perched on the roof. I think the bird was a _____.
8. There will be a short _____, and then we will start the second part of the play.

☐ Correct

I. **Practice Activity 3.** Fill in each blank with the best word.

1. If you take things out of a box, you _____ the box.
   untie / unpack / unleash

2. If you cannot speak, you are _____.
   nameless / speechless / endless

3. If you tell people about something, you make a _____.
   refill / repay / report

4. If something can hurt you, it is _____.
   harmful / boastful / handful

5. If you can take something from room to room, it is _____.
   fixable / preventable / portable

6. If a painting looks like you, it is a good _____.
   freshness / madness / likeness

☐ Correct   ☐ Checking Up

27

LESSON 7

■ **New Sound.** Say the words.

<u>oi</u>l   j<u>oy</u>

A. **New Words.** Say each sound. Say each word.

1. b<u>oi</u>l   b<u>oy</u>   p<u>oi</u>nt
2. p<u>ai</u>nt   R<u>oy</u>   p<u>aw</u>n
3. j<u>oy</u>   s<u>oi</u>l   g<u>oo</u>se
4. c<u>oi</u>n   c<u>oo</u>l   n<u>oi</u>se

5. Turn the heat higher if you want to boil the broth.
6. Roy is the name of my horse.
7. The rose will grow better in potting soil.
8. This car makes a lot of noise.

B. **Challenge Words.** Say the words.

turmoil   employ   enjoy   destroy   tinfoil
  1 2   1 2   1 2   1   2   1   2

boycott   joyride   oyster   appointment   sharpshooter
 1   2   1   2   1 2   1   2   3   1   2   3

C. **Word Parts.** Say the words.

<u>be</u>come   <u>de</u>lay   frac<u>tion</u>

D. **Words with Word Parts.** Say the words.

1. <u>be</u>side   <u>de</u>frost   <u>pre</u>sent   <u>re</u>think
2. ac<u>tion</u>   men<u>tion</u>   cool<u>ness</u>   tooth<u>less</u>
3. <u>be</u>long<u>ing</u> <u>de</u>ten<u>tion</u> <u>de</u>vo<u>tion</u> <u>re</u>flec<u>tion</u>

E. **Sight Words.** Say the words.

old   cold   told   gold   sold
one   other   many   another   about
want   all   there   come   what

F. **Passages.** Read each part of the story. Write the story part number under the picture that goes with each story part.

Roy's Coolness

Part 1

"I am sick of this! Day after day we sit in this room for no good reason. I want to play and have fun. That's not too much to ask for, is it, Will?" said Sweet Thing.

"Hush, hush, Sweet Thing," Will said. "If you make too much noise, Roy will wake up. That would destroy it for all of us. Besides, we still have each other. Let's enjoy what we can and not mention what we can't fix. There, there, don't cry," said the old sharpshooter.

"I feel the same way," Bess said. "For a long time, I sat right next to Roy's bed. Now I am with you in the dark, like a discarded dishrag. What's the point of this?" Bess said with a sniff. With that, the toys all went to sleep.

Part 2

The boy named Roy woke up at six the next day. He put on his shirt and jeans and dashed from the room.

"What could be *that* important?" asked Bess. "It's just six. He treats us as if we are just toys, and I am not a toy! I am a bank with lots of bright coins in me. If he has no interest in his other toys, these coins of mine could get him a *good* toy to play with," said Bess.

"What do you mean by a 'good' toy?" yelled Sweet Thing. "I am a paint-by-number kit, and I have many good drawings left!"

"That's right," said the pawn from the chess set. "We are all good toys and games. There must be another reason for Roy not to play with us."

Part 3

"Come, come," said the old sharpshooter. "This will not help us at all. Roy may have an appointment to keep."

"I can't help it," said Sweet Thing. "Bess makes me boiling mad! Roy kept that bank by his bed for a long time. Just because of that, she thinks she is better than the rest of us." For a while, no toy spoke. Then Sweet Thing said, "Besides, Roy may have had one appointment today, but that can't explain his actions these past three weeks. I think he is boycotting us. What can he be doing with his time?" she asked with a sigh.

G. **Practice Activity 1.** Read each question. Look back at the story on page 29. Fill in each blank with the best word.

Part 1

1. **WHERE** were the toys?

    The toys were in a _____.

2. **WHAT** did Sweet Thing want to do?

    She wanted to _____ and have _____.

3. **WHO** owned the toys?

    The toys belonged to _____.

Part 2

4. **WHAT** did Roy do in the morning?

    Roy put on his _____ and _____ and dashed from the room.

5. **WHAT** was Bess?

    Bess was a _____.

6. **WHAT** was Sweet Thing?

    Sweet Thing was a _____-by-_____ kit.

Part 3

7. **HOW** long had Roy not played with his toys?

    Roy had not played with his toys for _____ _____.

8. **WHAT** did Sweet Thing think Roy was doing to the toys?

    Sweet Thing thought that Roy was _____ the _____.

☐ Correct

H. **Practice Activity 2.** Read the story. Fill in each blank with the best word.

On Mom's birthday, Roy said, "I am going to bake a cake for Mom. I will just follow the directions on the box. I hope Mom enjoys her birthday cake."

DIRECTIONS
1. **Boil a cup of water.**
2. **Put the cake mix into a bowl.**
3. **Stir the boiling water into the cake mix.**
4. **Spoon the mix into a pan.**

1. Roy wanted to make a _____ cake for Mom.
   birthday   direction   spoon

2. First, Roy had to _____ a cup of water.
   soil   stir   boil

3. Then he had to put the cake mix into a _____.
   boil   bowl   pan

4. Next, he had to _____ the water into the cake mix.
   boil   spoon   stir

5. Roy put the cake into the stove to _____.
   rake   make   bake

6. Roy said, "I hope Mom will _____ her birthday cake."
   paint   cool   enjoy

☐ Correct

I. **Practice Activity 3.** Fill in each blank with the better word.

1. Mark did not _____ that he would be late.
   He did say that he had work to finish.
   fraction
   mention

2. The storm will _____ the train.
   The train will be very late.
   defrost
   delay

3. The breeze at the beach was very cool.
   Because of the _____, I put on a jacket.
   toothless
   coolness

4. Tom could not tell us much. He was _____.
   speechless
   smoothness

5. You can take the TV to the basement. The TV is _____.
   likeable
   portable

6. I can see my _____ in the pool.
   reflection
   detention

☐ Correct

31

LESSON 8

A. New Words. Say each sound. Say each word.

1. j<u>oi</u>n   j<u>ai</u>l   t<u>oy</u>
2. t<u>ea</u>   sp<u>oi</u>l   t<u>oi</u>l
3. m<u>au</u>l   Fl<u>oy</u>d   sp<u>oo</u>l
4. m<u>oi</u>st   cr<u>aw</u>l   Tr<u>oy</u>
5. It's fun to join a club during the summer.
6. The hot sun may spoil the ripe bananas.
7. Will Floyd drive to Florida next week?
8. The rag must be moist for it to clean the spill.

B. Challenge Words. Say the words.

soybean (1 2)   noiseless (1 2)   annoy (1 2)   loiter (1 2)   exploit (1 2)

toyshop (1 2)   charcoal (1 2)   corduroy (1 2 3)   employee (1 2 3)   employer (1 2 3)

C. Word Parts. Say the words.

<u>be</u>come   <u>de</u>lay   frac<u>tion</u>

D. Words with Word Parts. Say the words.

1. <u>be</u>fore   <u>de</u>part   <u>pre</u>fer   <u>re</u>make
2. sec<u>tion</u>   late<u>ness</u>   light<u>ness</u>   por<u>tion</u>
3. <u>re</u><u>de</u>fine   <u>de</u>struc<u>tion</u>   <u>de</u>scrip<u>tion</u>   <u>pre</u>ven<u>tion</u>

E. Sight Words. Say the words.

old	fold	cold	told	hold
give	other	about	through	find
all	would	were	there	want

F. **Passages.** Read each part of the story. Write the story part number under the picture that goes with each story part.

Annoyed Toys

Part 1

The days seemed to crawl by, and still Roy showed no interest in his toys. There was a lot of gloom on the toy shelf. At times, Sweet Thing and Bess would fight, but the rest of the time, there was no noise at all. Roy came to his room to sleep, but that was all.

Floyd the Moose made an effort to teach the game of chess to Troy the Puppet, but it was no use. The pawn in the chess set liked to tease Troy. When Troy paused to think about his next play, the pawn would jump to a different spot.

These were long, long days for the sad toys.

Part 2

"I cannot take too much more of this," Bess said on a Thursday afternoon. "Roy is just spoiled. There's no other description that fits. Just because he has other things to do, he keeps us here like we were in jail. I would prefer that he give us to some other boy. We might give some joy to a different boy. Besides, I like to be needed, and I am sick of all this fighting. That's the way I feel about it."

"Well, what are we going to do about it?" asked Sweet Thing. "I agree with you. I am sick of all this fighting, too." The rest of the toys looked shocked. The old sharpshooter smiled a sad smile.

Part 3

The next day was much like the other days. Floyd the Moose and Troy the Puppet gave up trying to play chess. For a while they played a card game called Go Fish. "Give me all your fives," said Troy.

"What a feat!" yelled Floyd. "Did you sneak a peek? I'm through! You have all my cards!"

Just then they saw Roy. The toys became noiseless. Roy went over to the shelf and said to the toys, "I am very glad to see you all. Today was my last day in the school play. I joined the play because it seemed like it would be fun, but I had to spend a lot of time at school. I have missed playing with you." Roy stopped and then smiled as he reached for a toy. He said, "Because the play is over, I can spend more time with all of you!"

_____   _____   _____

G. **Practice Activity 1.** Read each question. Look back at the story on page 33. Fill in each blank with the best word.

Part 1

1. **WHY** was there gloom on the toy shelf?

   There was gloom on the toy shelf because Roy showed _____ _____ in his toys.

2. **WHAT** did Floyd try to do?

   He made an effort to teach the game of _____ to Troy.

3. **WHAT** did the pawn do during the chess game?

   The pawn would jump to a different _____.

Part 2

4. **WHAT** did Bess say about Roy?

   Bess said that Roy was _____.

5. **WHAT** did Bess want Roy to do?

   Bess wanted Roy to give the toys to some other _____.

Part 3

6. **WHAT** card game did Floyd and Troy play?

   They played _____ _____.

7. **WHY** had Roy not played with his toys?

   Roy had not played with his toys because he had joined a _____ _____.

8. **WHAT** will Roy do with his toys?

   Roy will spend more _____ with his toys.

☐ Correct

H. Practice Activity 2. Read the story. Fill in the blank with the best word or words.

On Beth's third birthday, her sister made a big, moist birthday cake for her. Her mom and dad gave her toys, a green shirt, and corduroy pants. Beth liked being spoiled on her birthday. After she ate birthday cake, Beth went to the backyard to play. With a big spoon, Beth dug a road in the garden for her cars and trucks.

1. It was Beth's _____ birthday.
   first   third   fifth

2. Beth's sister made her a _____.
   green shirt   moist cake   big toy

3. Her mom and dad gave her _____ pants.
   corduroy   green   yellow

4. Beth liked being _____ on her birthday.
   crawled   joined   spoiled

5. Beth went to play in the _____.
   bedroom   basement   backyard

6. With a spoon, Beth dug a _____ for her cars and trucks.
   boy   road   soil

☐ Correct

I. Practice Activity 3. Fill in each blank with the better word.

1. Jeff plans to be a fisherman. Jeff will _____ a fisherman. — before / become

2. The storm will make the train late. The storm will _____ the train. — delay / defrost

3. The test had three parts. It had three _____. — sections / mentions

4. The dress is too big for Jan. She will need to _____ the dress. — remake / rebake

5. The train will leave at six. It will _____ at six. — defrost / depart

6. The cake was very fresh. I liked the cake's _____. — lateness / freshness

7. The stool was next to the desk. It was _____ the desk. — beside / become

8. Doctors and nurses help us keep well. They like to _____ illness. — pretend / prevent

☐ Correct

35

LESSON 9

A. **New Words.** Say each sound. Say each word.

1. c<u>oi</u>l   c<u>oa</u>t   c<u>oy</u>
2. t<u>oy</u>   p<u>ai</u>nts   p<u>oi</u>nts
3. f<u>ai</u>l   f<u>oi</u>l   p<u>aw</u>n
4. t<u>oi</u>l   t<u>oo</u>l   p<u>oise</u>
5. Grease the coil so it will not rust.
6. The speaker gave us some important points to remember.
7. Should he put the chicken on a sheet of foil?
8. You will gain poise as you grow older.

B. **Challenge Words.** Say the words.

en·joy (1 2)   oint·ment (1 2)   poi·son (1 2)   con·voy (1 2)   broil·er (1 2)

a·void (1 2)   em·broi·der (1 2 3)   dis·ap·point (1 2 3)   de·stroy·er (1 2 3)   en·joy·ment (1 2 3)

C. **Word Parts.** Say the words.

<u>be</u>come   <u>de</u>lay   frac<u>tion</u>

D. **Words with Word Parts.** Say the words.

1. <u>de</u>cay   <u>be</u>long   <u>re</u>sold   <u>re</u>do
2. trac<u>tion</u>   wit<u>ness</u>   suc<u>tion</u>   sleep<u>less</u>
3. <u>de</u>duc<u>tion</u>   <u>be</u>moan<u>ing</u>   <u>re</u>ac<u>tion</u>   <u>un</u>men<u>tion</u><u>able</u>

E. **Sight Words.** Say the words.

old	cold	sold	fold	told
give	many	other	also	through
come	were	there	work	find

F. **Passages.** Read each part of the story. Write the story part number under the picture that goes with each story part.

Toys

Part 1

Where do toys come from? Many would say that toys come from toy stores or other big stores. Today many toys do come from stores. In the past, toys were made at home or by people called toymakers.

Toys made in the past were carved and painted by hand. Many toys today are made of plastic. They are different from past toys. They also may not last as long. In the past, people saved toys that they liked and passed them on to other children to play with.

Part 2

A toymaker must enjoy working with his or her hands. Toymakers must cut, saw, or carve each part of the toy by hand. They must also make all the parts fit. If the parts do not fit, the toymakers will have to redo some of them.

Tools like a saw or a drill can be helpful, but a toymaker's hands are the best tools. When a toy is all made, the toymaker may sand it to make it smooth and then paint it. The work takes time but gives joy to the toymaker. Toymakers think it is time well spent because they can give such joy to children.

Part 3

Making toys for children to play with and enjoy is an art and a craft. Many people who make toys sell them at arts and crafts shows. Most things at an arts and crafts show are made by hand.

People like toys that have been made with devotion. Toys made by hand may cost a bit more, but people understand that toymakers spent a lot of time and toil making them.

The next time you go to an arts and crafts show, look for a toymaker's booth. You may find toys that were made by hand, like a boat to float in a tub.

  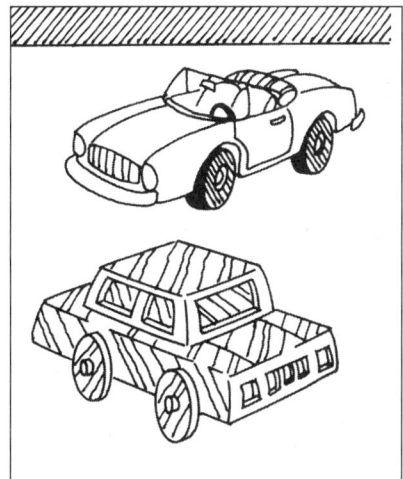

G. **Practice Activity 1.** Read each question. Look back at the story on page 37. Fill in each blank with the best word.

Part 1

1. **WHO** made toys in the past?

    In the past, _____ made toys.

2. **WHAT** are many toys made of today?

    Today many toys are made of _____.

3. **WHAT** did people do with toys in the past, since the toys lasted longer?

    People saved the toys and passed them on to other _____.

Part 2

4. **WHAT** are a toymaker's best tools?

    A toymaker's _____ are the best tools.

5. **HOW** might toymakers finish a toy?

    They might _____ it to make it smooth and then

    _____ it.

6. **WHY** do toymakers enjoy making toys?

    They enjoy making toys because the toys give such _____

    to children.

Part 3

7. **WHERE** can you find handmade toys today?

    You can find handmade toys at an _____ and

    _____ show.

8. **WHY** do people like handmade toys?

    People like handmade toys because the toys are made with _____.

☐ Correct

H. Practice Activity 2. Underline the endings that make sense.

1. On a hot afternoon, Carl might _____.
   a. enjoy a trip to the beach
   b. see a raccoon in the moonlight
   c. cut the lawn with his lawn mower
   d. stay in the shade to avoid a sunburn

2. On a dark night, Janis might _____.
   a. sit inside and embroider a pillowcase
   b. get a suntan at the beach
   c. enjoy an oyster dinner
   d. play her autoharp and sing

☐ Correct

I. Practice Activity 3. Fill in each blank with the best word.

sleepless	before	destroy	redo	prefer	handful
likeness	decay	sections	belong	mention	readable

1. Did you tell Jan that slacks are on sale? Did you _____ that corduroy slacks are on sale?

2. I like hot dogs better than hamburgers. I _____ hot dogs.

3. The box had five parts. It had five _____.

4. The report had lots of mistakes. Janis had to _____ the report.

5. These toys are Beth's. The toys _____ to Beth.

6. The drawing looks very much like Pam. It is a close _____.

7. I did not sleep last night. It was a _____ night.

8. First we will make coleslaw. Then we will make hamburgers. We will make the coleslaw _____ we make the hamburgers.

9. My handwriting is so messy. It is not very _____.

10. If you do not clean your teeth, they will _____.

11. My little sister gathered a _____ of small shells.

12. An untended fire can _____ a forest.

☐ Correct   ☐ Checking Up

39

LESSON 10

■ **New Sound.** Say the word.

n<u>ew</u>

A. New Words. Say each sound. Say each word.

1. n<u>ew</u> n<u>oi</u>se gr<u>ew</u>
2. gr<u>ai</u>n ch<u>ew</u> st<u>ew</u>
3. n<u>ew</u>s f<u>ee</u> d<u>ew</u>
4. dr<u>aw</u>n dr<u>ew</u> fl<u>ew</u>
5. Is that a new hair band?
6. I like stew made of beef, green beans, and corn.
7. The dew on the leaves of the tree was shining.
8. The bird flew to its nest in the beech tree.

B. Challenge Words. Say the words.

| jewel | newsstand | newscast | chewable | New York |
| 1 2 | 1   2 | 1 2 | 1   2 | 1   2 |

| newspaper | screwdriver | newsletter | subscribe | storekeeper |
| 1 2 3 | 1 2 3 | 1 2 3 | 1 2 | 1 2 3 |

C. Word Parts. Say the words.

<u>in</u>spect   <u>ex</u>pand   bad<u>ly</u>   wind<u>y</u>

D. Words with Word Parts. Say the words.

1. <u>in</u>fect <u>in</u>flate <u>de</u>mand <u>ex</u>port
2. night<u>ly</u> luck<u>y</u> like<u>ly</u> reason<u>able</u>
3. <u>in</u>spec<u>tion</u> <u>ex</u>act<u>ly</u> <u>ex</u>plain<u>able</u> <u>in</u>fec<u>tion</u>

E. Sight Words. Say the words.

find	mind	kind		
over	give	told	about	another
what	who	could	come	now	good

F. **Passages.** Read each part of the story. Write the story part number under the picture that goes with each story part.

School Reporters

Part 1

Kris liked Miss Sanchez's class. But today he could not wait for the class to end. At the end of class, Miss Sanchez was going to say who would work on the school newspaper. Kris and some of the others had been waiting all week for this news.

At last Miss Sanchez said, "Boys and girls, I have some good news and some bad news. The good news is that nine of you asked me about being on the newspaper staff. The bad news is that we need just three more people. It was too hard for me to choose just three of you. I have come up with a plan that I hope you will all like. Let me tell you about it."

Part 2

After class, Kris and some others sat down on the school's steps to chat about Miss Sanchez's plan. "What a drag!" Kris said to Beth and Liz. "Who needs another paper to do? Miss Sanchez has seen what we can do. She could have drawn names from a hat if she had too many people to choose from." Kris groaned. "Another paper is all I need!"

"Be reasonable, Kris," Liz said. "If you stop to think about it, it's the best way to show that you are the best person to work on the newspaper. Keep in mind that if Miss Sanchez just drew names, being chosen to work on the newspaper would be *luck*, not *skill*. Besides, your name may not have been drawn."

"That's right, Kris. We have a week to find a topic for a paper. It will have to be good, so let's start thinking about *that*."

Part 3

During the week, Kris, Beth, and Liz met many times at Kris's home to discuss the newspaper reports that they had to turn in soon. Kris had yet to start. "I can't help it," Kris said. "This is a slow news week. I need to find exactly the right thing to do my paper on. It has to have a new and different approach. It will come to me. Wait and see," he said.

"Do not wait too long, Kris," Beth said. "We have to turn these papers in next Thursday. Besides, Miss Sanchez said that a good news reporter *finds* news. You can't just wait for it to come to you. I have to go home. Good luck."

G. Practice Activity 1. Read each question. Look back at the story on page 41. Fill in each blank with the best word.

Part 1

1. Why did Kris want class to end?

    Kris wanted class to end because Miss Sanchez was going to say who could join the _____ _____.

2. Why didn't Miss Sanchez say who would be working on the newspaper staff?

    Miss Sanchez said it was too hard to _____ just three people.

Part 2

3. What did Miss Sanchez ask the boys and girls to do next?

    Miss Sanchez asked them to write another _____.

4. How did Kris want Miss Sanchez to choose the new staff members?

    Kris wanted Miss Sanchez to draw _____ from a hat.

5. What did Kris need to do in the next week?

    Kris had to find a _____ for his paper.

Part 3

6. What reason did Kris give for not picking a topic?

    Kris said that it was a _____ _____ week.

7. What kind of approach did Kris want his paper to have?

    Kris wanted his paper to have a _____ and _____ approach.

8. What did Miss Sanchez say about a good news reporter?

    Miss Sanchez said that a good news reporter _____ news.

☐ Correct

H. **Practice Activity 2.** Fill in each blank with the better word or words.

1. The _____ will pay her _____ this Thursday.
   employees
   storekeeper

2. The employer will _____ in the _____.
   newspaper
   advertise

3. Do you _____ to a _____?
   newspaper
   subscribe

4. Where is the _____ story about the _____ pills?
   newspaper
   chewable

5. The _____ put the _____ in the display case.
   jewels
   storekeeper

6. Jane got a _____ from the _____ chest.
   screwdriver
   tool

7. In the morning, I picked up a _____ at the _____.
   newsstand
   newspaper

8. Last summer, I went _____ in _____.
   sightseeing
   New York

☐ Correct

I. **Practice Activity 3.** Fill in each blank with the best word.

nightly   **badly**   **demand**   **lucky**
inspect   **expert**   **windy**   **expand**

1. If the wind blows, it is _____.
2. If you have lots of luck, you are _____.
3. If you look at something with care, you _____ it.
4. If you are very, very good at something, you are an _____ at it.
5. If you ask for something that you want, you might _____ it.
6. If something happens each night, it happens _____.
7. If you did a bad job on a task, you did it _____.
8. If a balloon got bigger and bigger, it would _____.

☐ Correct

LESSON 11

A. New Words. Say each sound. Say each word.

1. ch<u>ew</u>   p<u>aw</u>   thr<u>ew</u>
2. cr<u>ew</u>   j<u>oi</u>n   bl<u>ew</u>
3. gr<u>ew</u>   br<u>ew</u>   sh<u>ow</u>n
4. j<u>oy</u>   cr<u>aw</u>l   shr<u>ew</u>
5. Chew your food well when you eat.
6. The wind blew the rain through the screen door.
7. The storekeeper will brew a pot of tea for the staff meeting.
8. In my garden, I saw a shrew, three green bugs, and one crow.

B. Challenge Words. Say the words.

sewer (1 2)   cashew (1 2)   unscrew (1 2)   mildew (1 2)   newborn (1 2)

newsreel (1 2)   crewneck (1 2)   seaplane (1 2)   jeweler (1 2 3)   authorize (1 2 3)

C. Word Parts. Say the words.

<u>in</u>spect   <u>ex</u>pand   bad<u>ly</u>   wind<u>y</u>

D. Words with Word Parts. Say the words.

1. <u>be</u>moan   <u>in</u>tend   <u>de</u>pend   <u>ex</u>claim
2. nois<u>y</u>   sand<u>y</u>   bright<u>ly</u>   slow<u>ly</u>
3. <u>in</u>ven<u>tion</u>   <u>de</u>light<u>ful</u>   <u>ex</u>pert<u>ly</u>   <u>pre</u>scrip<u>tion</u>

E. Sight Words. Say the words.

find   mind   kind

give   over   mother   one

told   your   about

where   many   why

F. Passages. Read each part of the story. Write the story part number under the picture that goes with each story part.

A Nose for News

Part 1

During the week, Kris spent a lot of time with pen and paper in hand. One by one he threw the papers into the trash can. "Chewing your pen like that will not help, Kris," his mother said one night. "There's not much time left," she said as she turned the TV on. "Let's see what is on the nightly news. You might find that helpful." The TV news team reported on a big brush fire, a new car invention, and a seaplane that had crashed not far from the local beach.

"That's it!" Kris exclaimed. He started to grin. "I should have turned the TV on yesterday," he said. "Thanks, Mom. I can depend on you when I need to unscrew my brain!"

Part 2

On Thursday, Kris joined Liz and Beth on the steps of the school. They each had a paper to turn in to Miss Sanchez. "It's about time," Liz said to Kris. "I see you have your paper. What's it about?" she asked brightly.

"You will have to wait and see," Kris said. "I admit that's a rotten thing to say, but I intend to keep still about it," he said with a grin. "Miss Sanchez said she would read them all in class. You will have to wait until then."

Liz and Beth looked at each other and smiled. "OK, Kris," Liz said. "Have it your way. We will all wait until Miss Sanchez reads them. Let's go—class is about to start."

Part 3

"Well, boys and girls, the time has come to read these papers. After I read them all to you, I will ask you to vote for the top three. That will help me pick the new school reporters. As I read, remember the important points that each report should mention: who, what, where, when, and why." Then Miss Sanchez started to read the papers.

Beth's paper was all about the food served at school. The paper Liz turned in was about the school play. Another paper was about the new fire station down the street. One paper was on the art show in the park.

At last, Miss Sanchez got to Kris's paper. It was all about the seaplane crash. The crew of the boat that had towed the plane to shore had given Kris the facts. When Miss Sanchez finished Kris's story, everyone clapped and smiled at Kris. After the class had voted, Kris was one of the new reporters.

G. **Practice Activity 1.** Read each question. Look back at the story on page 45. Fill in each blank with the best word.

Part 1

1. Where did Kris throw his many papers while trying to begin his story?

   He threw many papers into the _____ _____.

2. What did Kris's mother tell him to look at?

   She told him to look at the _____ _____ on TV.

Part 2

3. Where did Kris meet Liz and Beth?

   He met them on the _____ of the _____.

4. What did the children have?

   They each had a _____ to turn in to Miss Sanchez.

Part 3

5. What important points did the papers need to mention?

   The papers had to tell _____, _____,

   _____, _____, and _____.

6. What was Beth's paper about?

   Beth's paper was about the _____ served at _____.

7. What was Kris's paper about?

   His paper was about the _____ _____.

8. Who gave Kris the facts for his paper?

   The _____ of the _____ that had towed the plane

   to shore had given Kris the facts for his paper.

☐ Correct

46

H. **Practice Activity 2.** Fill in each blank with the better word.

1. The _____ locked the _____ in the display case.
   jeweler
   jewels

2. The _____ left his _____ baby with his babysitter.
   newborn
   gardener

3. I asked the _____ for a _____ and a hammer.
   storekeeper
   screwdriver

4. Barb gets lots of _____ from reading the _____.
   enjoyment
   newspaper

5. The first _____ was about a _____ pipe that broke during the night.
   sewer
   newscast

6. After dinner we had a _____ nut pie and _____.
   cashew
   coffee

7. The bad grade on the _____ will _____ Troy.
   disappoint
   assignment

8. Floyd _____ his ride on the _____.
   enjoyed
   seaplane

☐ Correct

I. **Practice Activity 3.** Fill in each blank with the best word.

intend   delightful   depend   sandy   noisy   invention   brightly   slowly

1. If you go to the beach, you are likely to get _____.
2. If there is lots of noise in a room, the room is _____.
3. If you invent something, it is an _____.
4. If the moon is bright, it shines _____.
5. If a car will not go fast, it will go _____.
6. If you need a person very much, you _____ on him or her.
7. If you plan to do something, you _____ to do it.
8. If you had a fun time at a party, you might say you had a _____ time.

☐ Correct

47

LESSON 12

A. New Words. Say each sound. Say each word.

1. fl<u>ew</u>   p<u>aws</u>   bl<u>ew</u>
2. n<u>ew</u>   shr<u>ew</u>   pr<u>oo</u>f
3. n<u>ews</u>   str<u>ea</u>m   dr<u>ew</u>
4. thr<u>ew</u>   str<u>ew</u>n   j<u>oy</u>s
5. A black crow flew over the wheat crop.
6. The shrew hid under the bush when the cat came into the yard.
7. I had a dream that I was on the news.
8. Who threw this red brick through the window?

B. Challenge Words. Say the words.

newsstand (1 2)   Lewis (1 2)   sewer (1 2)   dewdrop (1 2)   August (1 2)

newsprint (1 2)   frustrate (1 2)   classmates (1 2)   proofread (1 2)   appointment (1 2 3)

C. Word Parts. Say the words.

<u>in</u>spect   <u>ex</u>pand   bad<u>ly</u>   wind<u>y</u>

D. Words with Word Parts. Say the words.

1. <u>in</u>form   <u>ex</u>tend   <u>de</u>feat   <u>un</u>real
2. snow<u>y</u>   hard<u>ly</u>   plen<u>ty</u>   dark<u>ness</u>
3. <u>ex</u>tinc<u>tion</u>   <u>in</u>sight<u>ful</u>   <u>pre</u>dic<u>tion</u>   <u>un</u>help<u>ful</u>

E. Sight Words. Say the words.

find   mind   kind

over   give   told   other   another

through   want   all   about   many

F. **Passages.** Read each part of the story. Write the story part number under the picture that goes with each story part.

The Newsstand

Part 1

17 After school, Kris met with Beth and Liz at the new record store. "You did it, Kris," said Liz. "We are so happy for you!"
25 "Thank you," said Kris. "I can't wait to start my job as a news reporter. You were
42 right, Beth. A news reporter has to *find* the news rather than waiting for it to happen. I
60 have a plan that will help me be the best news reporter the school has had."

Part 2

76 Later that week, Kris went to see Mrs. Drew at the *Daily Free News*. "Mrs. Drew, " Kris
93 said, "I would like to join your news crew. I am a news reporter at school. I want to
112 report important news to my school. This is the best way to get up-to-date news."
127 "That's a smart plan," said Mrs. Drew. "I would like to have you work with my news
143 crew. But, I have another plan that may be more helpful to you." Kris's smile grew wide.

Part 3

160 Liz and Beth were jogging down Dew Street on Saturday morning when they saw Kris
175 standing in a corner newsstand. "Kris, what are you *doing*?" asked Beth.
187 "I am working for Mrs. Drew at the *Daily Free News*. I work at this newsstand selling
204 newspapers from all over each Saturday morning. Mrs. Drew said that I could read and
219 keep all the newspapers I want! You are speaking with one news reporter who will keep
235 the school newspaper up-to-date!"

239

G. **Practice Activity 1.** Read each question. Look back at the story on page 49. Fill in each blank with the best word.

Part 1

1. Where did Kris, Liz, and Beth meet after school?

   They met at the new _____ _____.

2. What did Kris have that would make him the best reporter the school had had?

   Kris had a _____ about how to be the best reporter.

Part 2

3. Who met with Kris later that week?

   Kris met with _____ _____.

4. Where was this meeting?

   The meeting was at the _____ _____ _____.

5. What did Kris want to join?

   Kris wanted to join the _____ _____.

Part 3

6. Where did Liz and Beth find Kris on Saturday morning?

   They found Kris standing in a corner _____ on _____ _____.

7. What did Kris get to keep from the newsstand?

   Kris got to keep all the _____ he wanted.

8. Why was Kris happy about working in the newsstand?

   Kris was happy because he can keep the school's _____ up-to-date.

☐ Correct

H. Practice Activity 2. Fill in each blank with the better word.

1. Jane got a _____ at the _____.
   newsstand
   newspaper

2. On a hot _____ day, it is fun to go _____.
   sightseeing
   August

3. Liz's _____ went to the _____ at 12:00.
   lunchroom
   classmates

4. The _____ sells hammers and _____.
   screwdrivers
   salesperson

5. _____ likes to eat _____ nuts and peanuts.
   Lewis
   cashew

6. When Lewis could not _____ the top on the jar, he got very _____.
   frustrated
   unscrew

☐ Correct

I. Practice Activity 3. Fill in each blank with the better word.

1. Barb will take a long time to draw the hawk.
   She will draw it _____.
   slowly
   brightly

2. The crew will take the crates off the truck.
   The crew will _____ the truck.
   unpile
   unload

3. Sam is very ill. He has a throat _____.
   infection
   invitation

4. Mr. Martin will tell the children how to do the task.
   He will _____ the directions.
   extend
   explain

5. Jan's soccer team will beat the High Kickers.
   Jan's team will _____ the High Kickers.
   defeat
   demand

6. Jane never gets to class on time. Her _____ upsets her teacher.
   darkness
   lateness

7. After dinner, Mark cleans the plates. His _____ job is to clean the plates.
   hardly
   nightly

8. Liz has many socks. Liz has _____ of socks.
   oily
   plenty

☐ Correct   ☐ Checking Up

LESSON 13

■ **New Sound.** Say the word.

l<u>ou</u>d

A. **New Words.** Say each sound. Say each word.

1. <u>ou</u>t　　　　j<u>oi</u>nt　　　　r<u>ou</u>nd
2. sh<u>aw</u>l　　　cl<u>ou</u>d　　　l<u>oo</u>se
3. h<u>ou</u>se　　　bl<u>ew</u>　　　sh<u>ou</u>t
4. pr<u>ou</u>d　　　bl<u>ou</u>se　　bl<u>ow</u>n
5. She needs the round ball of string.
6. That cloud looks like a muffin.
7. The people will shout when they see the star player.
8. Fred was proud of his schoolwork.

B. **Challenge Words.** Say the words.

counter　　thousand　　surround　　countless　　southwest
 1   2　　 1   2　　　 1   2　　　 1   2　　　 1   2

doghouse　　outburst　　trousers　　outspoken　　encounter
 1   2　　　1   2　　　 1   2　　　1   2   3　　 1   2   3

C. **Word Parts.** Say the words.

<u>con</u>tain　　　jo<u>yous</u>

D. **Words with Word Parts.** Say the words.

1. <u>con</u>sists　　<u>ex</u>pect　　　<u>in</u>spect　　<u>con</u>sider　　<u>be</u>came　　<u>re</u>sults
2. fam<u>ous</u>　　　atten<u>tion</u>　　tremend<u>ous</u>　simp<u>ly</u>　　　use<u>ful</u>　　nerv<u>ous</u>
3. <u>con</u>struc<u>tion</u>　<u>ex</u>plain<u>able</u>　<u>in</u>forma<u>tion</u>　<u>dis</u>astr<u>ous</u>

E. **Sight Words.** Say the words.

walk　　　talk

coming　　woman　　even　　　now　　　kind

want　　　about　　　another　　cold　　　some

F. **Passages.** Read each part of the story. Write the story part number under the picture that goes with each story part.

The Grant Ranch

Part 1

"I want to stop on the way back and see Mrs. Grant," Will said to his boy seated in the wagon next to him. "I expect to have some time next week after the crops are all picked. She may need some help," he said.

"Why would a woman live way out there on that ranch? The kids at school say they have even seen her in trousers. She's kind of different, isn't she, Dad?" Tom asked.

Will grinned. "Nell Grant is an outspoken woman who works hard. That ranch is all she has, and she considers it home. She's proud of her house, too. She is a widow and her children are grown. She has worked hard to keep that old ranch. I think she has a lot of backbone," he said with a smile.

Part 2

When they got to Mrs. Grant's ranch, she was sitting on the porch. Tom was disappointed to see that she had on a blouse, skirt, and a shawl, not trousers. She greeted them and asked them to join her for tea. They all went into the house and sat down.

"What's new, Nell?" Will asked. "I have some time next week if I could be useful around here."

"Thanks, Will. I will keep that in mind, but right now I'm making out OK. I would have a lot more time if that loudmouth Bob Drake would stop pestering me to sell out to him. He wants that land on the southwest corner of the ranch. I have turned him down a thousand times, but he keeps coming back." Then she grinned. "I think I stopped him cold in his tracks today!" she said.

Part 3

"Have another cup of tea while I tell you about it," she said. "You will enjoy this. He was sitting right where you are. I was paying attention, sort of. Then he told me he was simply trying to help an old woman! I jumped up and shouted at him to leave. My outburst surprised him, to say the least. I hope he stays lost for a while," Nell said.

She went to the window and looked out. "I hate to rush you off, but it looks like a storm is brewing out there. You best go before you and Tom get soaked. Thanks for stopping. I will see you soon."

They thanked her for the tea and left. It was starting to rain.

G. **Practice Activity 1.** Read each question. Look back at the story on page 53. Fill in each blank with the best word.

Part 1

1. Whom did Will and Tom visit?

   They visited _____ _____.

2. Why did the children think that Mrs. Grant was different?

   The children said that they had seen Mrs. Grant in _____.

3. Why did Mrs. Grant have to work hard?

   She had to work hard to _____ the old ranch.

Part 2

4. What did Mrs. Grant ask Tom and Will?

   She asked them to join her for _____.

5. Why was Bob Drake pestering Mrs. Grant?

   Bob Drake wanted the _____ corner of the _____.

6. Did Nell sell the land to Bob Drake?

   No, she _____ him down a thousand times.

Part 3

7. What did Nell do when Bob Drake said he was simply trying to help an old woman?

   Nell asked Bob Drake to _____.

8. Why did Will and Tom have to leave?

   They had to leave because a _____ was brewing.

☐ Correct

H. **Practice Activity 2.** Fill in each blank with the better word.

1. At the diner, Ann sat on a _____ at the _____. — counter / stool

2. Fred will _____ his _____ in the sink. — trousers / launder

3. The _____ hid in the _____ when the boys came. — doghouse / raccoon

4. More than a _____ plants grew in the _____. — thousand / greenhouse

5. Stacks of lumber _____ the _____. — sawmill / surround

7. There were _____ newspapers stacked next to the _____. — countless / newsstand

☐ Correct

I. **Practice Activity 3.** Fill in each blank with the better word.

1. There are three toys in the box. The box _____ three toys. — contains / consider

2. Liz had lots of fun on her birthday. It was a _____ time for Liz. — joyous / disastrous

3. All of the boys will be on the soccer team. The coach will _____ all of the boys on the team. — include / intend

4. Tom will be home this afternoon. I _____ him at 3:00 P.M. — expect / extend

5. For three weeks, Pam painted the farmhouse. She painted very _____. — simply / slowly

6. Jan got 95 points on her test. She was pleased with the _____. — results / remake

7. The noise grew in the classroom. The teacher said, "I need your _____." — portion / attention

☐ Correct

LESSON 14

A. **New Words.** Say each sound. Say each word.

1. <u>ou</u>r   <u>oi</u>l   s<u>ou</u>nd
2. cl<u>ou</u>d   cl<u>aw</u>   s<u>ou</u>th
3. gr<u>ou</u>nd   m<u>ou</u>se   sc<u>oo</u>t
4. m<u>oi</u>st   sc<u>ou</u>t   h<u>ou</u>nd
5. Our cabin sits beside a lake.
6. Pat plans to go south.
7. Clark planted grass seed in the ground.
8. The scout threw water on the campfire.

B. **Challenge Words.** Say the words.

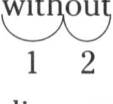 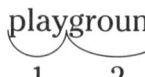 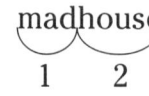 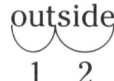 

without   playground   madhouse   outside   cloudless
 1 2   1   2   1   2   1 2   1   2

discount   thundercloud   underground   southwestern   fellowship
 1 2   1 2 3   1 2 3   1 2 3   1 2 3

C. **Word Parts.** Say the words.

<u>con</u>tain   joy<u>ous</u>

D. **Words with Word Parts.** Say the words.

1. <u>con</u>duct   <u>be</u>gan   <u>de</u>pends   <u>de</u>tails   <u>di</u>stant   <u>con</u>fess
2. glamor<u>ous</u>   happ<u>y</u>   sudden<u>ly</u>   horrend<u>ous</u>   collec<u>tion</u>   life<u>less</u>
3. <u>pre</u>dict<u>able</u>   <u>con</u>nect<u>able</u>   <u>in</u>teres<u>ting</u>   <u>re</u>turn<u>able</u>

E. **Sight Words.** Say the words.

walk   talk

warm   woman   even   over   kind

also   through   went   mother   give

F. **Passages.** Read each part of the story. Write the story part number under the picture that goes with each story part.

The Storm

Part 1

Will and Tom went south on Scout Trail. The rain was still light, but dark thunderclouds were all around. The horse pawed the ground at the sound of the distant thunder. "I hope we get home before those clouds burst," Tom said.

"We will do our best," Will said. "A lot depends on the horse and the rain. In the meantime, what did you think of your encounter with Nell Grant?" he said.

"She is an interesting woman. I wish I had been a mouse in the room when she shouted at Bob Drake." Suddenly, time ran out, and the storm was upon them.

Part 2

"You two are sopping wet!" Mother said as Will and Tom ran into the house. "Sit by the fire and get warm. The storm came up fast. Did you stop to see Nell? How is she?" Mom asked. They spoke of Nell Grant for a while. Will kept getting up to look out the window.

At last he said, "I can't help thinking about the crops and the livestock, too. This storm is awful. Nell Grant's ranch will also be hit hard. Her barn is in bad shape. Wind and rain like this could have disastrous results. Let's hope it stops soon. We may as well go to bed. There will be a lot of work to do in the morning."

Part 3

When Will checked his land the next morning, things were not as bad as they could have been. The roof of the barn was new, and that was a big help. Just before noon he said, "I think I will ride over to see Mrs. Grant and her barn. Do you want to come, Tom?" Tom nodded.

They rode around the back way, through the southwest corner of the Grant Ranch. Will stopped suddenly. The old tool shed looked like it had sunk into the ground, and Nell was sitting on the wet dirt by the shed.

Will and Tom rode closer. Nell turned to them and waved. "Oil. It's oil!" she said. "That's why Bob Drake wanted this land! The storm did something to the ground. I am going to be rich, Will! I can even get the barn fixed up right. Wait until I see Bob Drake," she said with a smile.

G. **Practice Activity 1.** Read each question. Look back at the story on page 57. Fill in each blank with the best word.

Part 1

1. Where did Will and Tom go when they left Mrs. Grant's ranch?

   They went south on _____ _____.

2. What did Tom hope?

   He hoped that they would get home before the _____ burst.

3. What did Tom say about Nell Grant?

   Tom said that she was an _____ woman.

Part 2

4. What did Tom and Will do when they got home?

   They sat down by the _____.

5. What was Will thinking about during the storm?
   Will was thinking about the _____ and the _____ and Mrs. Grant's barn.

Part 3

6. Where did Tom and Will go after checking the barn?

   They went to Mrs. Grant's _____.

7. Where was Mrs. Grant?

   Mrs. Grant was sitting on the wet _____ by the

   _____.

8. Why did Bob Drake want the land?

   He wanted the land because there was _____ in the ground.

☐ Correct

H. **Practice Activity 2.** Fill in each blank with the better word.

1. The _____ left _____ the case of jewels.
   without
   salesperson

2. After _____ class, the children went to the _____.
   playground
   drawing

3. The _____ smiled when she saw the _____ sky.
   cloudless
   farmer

4. The subway went _____ into a dark _____.
   underground
   tunnel

5. The dark sky filled with _____ of _____.
   thunderclouds
   thousands

6. The _____ gave a _____ of $1.00 for each can of coffee.
   discount
   storekeeper

☐ Correct

I. **Practice Activity 3.** Fill in each blank with the better word.

1. Mrs. Smith is the leader of the band. She will _____ the band tonight.
   conduct
   consists

2. Dennis was outstanding at tennis. He _____ famous for his tennis.
   began
   became

3. Janet put on the new dress. She looked very _____.
   glamorous
   famous

4. I think the criminal will tell about his crimes. I think he will _____ his crimes.
   confess
   contain

5. I count on my mom's help. I _____ on her.
   detail
   depend

6. The bike turned onto the highway next to a car. The car had to stop _____.
   brightly
   suddenly

7. Troy has a thousand shells in his display case. He has a big _____ of shells.
   collection
   attention

8. The rail went on and on. The trail was _____.
   lifeless
   endless

☐ Correct

LESSON 15

A. New Words. Say each sound. Say each word.

1. spr<u>ou</u>t   c<u>oa</u>ch   c<u>ou</u>ch
2. spr<u>aw</u>l   tr<u>ou</u>t   m<u>ou</u>th
3. h<u>au</u>l   gr<u>ou</u>ch   sp<u>ou</u>t
4. <u>ou</u>ch   thr<u>ew</u>   fl<u>our</u>
5. We sat down on our new couch.
6. Do you like fresh or frozen trout?
7. Turn off the bathtub spout.
8. "Ouch!" said Glen. "The horse nipped me."

B. Challenge Words. Say the words.

outgrew   dismount   farmhouse   account   countless
 1   2   1   2   1   2   1   2   1   2

Boy Scout   outlaw   scoutmaster   outstanding   counterclockwise
 1   2   1   2   1   2   3   1   2   3   1   2   3   4

C. Word Parts. Say the words.

<u>con</u>tain   joy<u>ous</u>

D. Words with Word Parts. Say the words.

1. <u>con</u>nect   <u>in</u>vite   <u>de</u>scribe   <u>re</u>sult   <u>ex</u>press   <u>con</u>tains
2. ad<u>dition</u>   enorm<u>ous</u>   direct<u>ly</u>   reason<u>able</u>   nerv<u>ous</u>   hungr<u>y</u>
3. <u>in</u>dustry   <u>con</u>trasting   <u>ex</u>act<u>ness</u>   <u>pre</u>dic<u>tion</u>

E. Sight Words. Say the words.

walk   talk

woman   women   over   even   warm

there   told   come   many   where

F. **Passages.** Read each part of the story. Write the story part number under the picture that goes with each story part.

The Lost Trout

Part 1

"I invited Ann and Mark over for dinner," Kris said to her husband. "Ann has the day off, and her kids are at camp this week. They have not even seen our new house yet."

"That sounds fine, Kris," Don said. "While you show Ann the house, I can tell Mark all about my fish. He will understand my disappointment. I just about had him, Kris. That fish was enormous!"

"Don, you have told that old fish tale a thousand times this week! The fish gets bigger each time you tell about it. At first it was just a trout. Soon you will be telling me it had a spout like a whale!" Kris grinned and left the room to start dinner.

Part 2

Don sat for a while, thinking about the famous lost trout. Then he went into the next room to find Kris. "OK, grouch, what can I do to help with dinner?" he asked with a smile.

"I have things well in hand," Kris said. "I will be happy if you simply clean off the couch and put out the snacks. We still have time before Ann and Mark get here."

Kris set the plates and dishes on the counter and turned on the broiler. When she went to find her husband, he was sprawled on the couch looking at a baseball game on TV. She joined him until they saw Ann and Mark come up the driveway.

Part 3

They all chatted for a while, and then they went outside to see the yard. When they went back in, Ann asked to see the rest of the new house. "Come with me, Ann," Kris said. "I will take you around and show it to you. Besides, that will give Don some time to tell his fish tale to Mark! He has been waiting for this all day," she said as they left the room.

Later, when Ann and Kris returned, Kris saw Don standing next to the couch. He was holding his arms three feet apart. "I am glad I fixed beef, and not fish, for dinner," Kris said with a grin. "I have had all the fish I can stand this week."

G. **Practice Activity 1.** Read each question. Look back at the story on page 61. Fill in each blank with the best word.

Part 1

1. Whom did Kris invite to dinner?

   Kris invited _____ and _____ to dinner.

2. What did Don want to tell Mark about?

   Don wanted to tell Mark about the _____ that got away.

3. What happened to the fish each time Don told the tale?

   The fish got _____ each time Don told the tale.

Part 2

4. What did Don do to help?

   He cleaned off the _____ and put out the _____.

5. What did Kris do?

   She set out the plates and dishes on the _____.

6. What did Kris and Don do while they waited for Ann and Mark?

   They looked at a _____ _____ on TV.

Part 3

7. What did Don tell Mark?

   Don told Mark his _____ _____.

8. How long was the famous lost fish this time?

   Don's famous lost fish was _____ feet long.

☐ Correct

62

H. **Practice Activity 2.** Fill in each blank with the better word.

1. Josh _____ the green _____ that he got for his third birthday.
   trousers
   outgrew

2. In the morning, the _____ cleaned the _____.
   farmhouse
   housekeeper

3. The Boy Scouts _____ the _____ up the trail.
   followed
   scoutmaster

4. There was much _____ when the _____ play ended.
   outstanding
   applause

5. The _____ has to _____ for each coin that she brings in.
   salesperson
   account

6. The gardener put the plants on the _____ inside the _____.
   counter
   greenhouse

☐ Correct

I. **Practice Activity 3.** Fill in each blank with the better word.

1. If a box has shells in it, the box _____ shells.
   connect
   contains

2. If you ask people to your house, you _____ them to your house.
   invite
   inspect

3. If you tell about something, you _____ it.
   describe
   depends

4. If you want some food, you are _____.
   hungry
   happy

5. If you tell about your feelings, you _____ your feelings.
   express
   exactly

6. If you want to find the sum of three numbers, you should use _____.
   collection
   addition

7. If something is very big, it is _____.
   joyous
   enormous

8. If you have to do something fast, you do it _____.
   brightly
   suddenly

☐ Correct   ☐ Checking Up

63

LESSON 16

■ **New Sounds.** Say the words.

<u>kn</u>ow   <u>ph</u>one   <u>qu</u>ack   <u>wr</u>ite

A. **New Words.** Say each sound. Say each word.

1. <u>kn</u>ot   <u>wr</u>eck   <u>qu</u>it
2. <u>kn</u>ight   <u>ph</u>one   <u>kn</u>ob
3. gra<u>ph</u>   <u>kn</u>ife   <u>wr</u>ote
4. <u>kn</u>eel   <u>qu</u>ilt   <u>wr</u>ap
5. Little girls and boys could wreck a neat room.
6. Turn the knob slowly so it will not squeak.
7. Draw the graph on the paper.
8. Will you display your quilt at the quilt show this fall?

B. **Challenge Words.** Say the words.

dolphin   wrapper   jackknife   shipwreck   knapsack
 1 2   1 2   1 2   1 2   1 2

knothole   vanquish   kneecap   underline   handwritten
 1 2   1 2   1 2   1 2 3   1 2 3

C. **Word Parts.** Say the words.

<u>c</u>omplete   hand<u>le</u>

D. **Words with Word Parts.** Say the words.

1. <u>c</u>ommand   <u>c</u>ompose   <u>c</u>onsult   <u>d</u>evelop   <u>in</u>deed   <u>b</u>eneath
2. sim<u>ple</u>   mid<u>dle</u>   tit<u>le</u>   empt<u>y</u>   rapid<u>ly</u>
3. <u>c</u>omplete<u>ly</u>   <u>c</u>onne<u>c</u>tion   <u>c</u>onsider<u>able</u>   <u>un</u>scram<u>ble</u>

E. **Sight Words.** Say the words.

don't   even   coming   find   two   sure

work   about   told   woman   give   machine

F. **Passages.** Read each part of the story. Write the story part number under the picture that goes with each story part.

The Time Machine

Part 1

"I am a nervous wreck, Trish!" Philip said as Trish reached for the knob. "This is the third time this week you have made me go in there with you. If Quay finds out . . . I can't even think about it!"

"I told you," Trish said, "that Quay is in her room on the phone. Besides, she thinks we are outside. I think I know how to work it. I saw the notes Quay wrote. It's simple." Trish looked at Philip in amazement. "Don't you understand? We give it the right command, and it takes us back in time. Just think what we can see and do. You can even pick the first date."

Part 2

"Are you nuts?" Philip yelled. "We don't even know if it works or not! For all you know, this time machine will split us into thousands of bits and even Quay will not know how to unscramble our parts."

"For your information," Trish said, "I *know* it works fine. Quay keeps detailed notes. Last week she sent a knife way back to 1939. It came back with a flick of Quay's wrist! The machine is completely safe."

Philip looked stunned. "A knife? Big deal! You want me to risk *my* life because a knife came back? Why do you think she is keeping this time machine under wraps? She still is not sure how it will work with *people*."

Part 3

"I have faith in Quay," Trish said. "Besides, I want to be the first woman to travel back in time. I also know just where I want to go. I long to have a knight kneel at my feet and kiss my hand." Trish giggled.

Philip and Trish discussed the time machine some more. At last, Trish said, "I understand how you feel, Philip, but I am willing to risk it. I will try it first. If I return safely, will you go with me next time?"

Philip said he would. Trish turned some knobs and consulted Quay's notes. Then with a knot in her throat, she said, "Wish me luck!"

G. **Practice Activity 1.** Read each question. Look back at the story on page 65. Fill in each blank with the best word.

Part 1

1. Who wanted to look at the time machine?

    _____ wanted to look at the time machine.

2. Whom did the time machine belong to?

    The time machine belonged to _____.

3. What is Trish letting Philip do?

    Trish is letting Philip pick the first _____.

Part 2

4. Why did Trish think the time machine would work?

    Last week Quay had sent a _____ back to 1939.

5. Why was Philip not sure that the time machine was safe?

    Philip was not sure how it would work with _____.

Part 3

6. Why did Trish want to go back in time?

    She wanted a _____ to kiss her hand.

7. Who was going to take the first ride in the time machine?

    _____ was going to take the first ride.

8. What did Trish say after she turned some knobs in the time machine?

    She said, "_____ _____ _____!"

☐ Correct

H. **Practice Activity 2.** Fill in each blank with the better word.

knapsack   jackknife   shipwreck   underline
wrapper   handwritten knothole   farmhouse

1. The _____ happened a mile off the coastline.
2. The _____ came off the box.
3. The Boy Scout put his _____ in his knapsack before the hike.
4. The reporter put his notepad in his _____.
5. Jean looked into the _____ in the tree.
6. The _____ stood on a hill surrounded by trees.
7. Barb will _____ the best words on the assignment.
8. The letter was _____.

☐ Correct

I. **Practice Activity 3.** Fill in each blank with the better word.

1. If you make film into prints, you _____ the film.   defrost / develop
2. If you finish a task, you _____ the task.   command / complete
3. If you do something very fast, you do it _____.   rapidly / slowly
4. If you make lots of noise, you are _____.   empty / noisy
5. If you are a member of a club, you _____ to the club.   beneath / belong
6. If a person is in front of you and a person is in back of you, you are in the _____.   middle / simple
7. If you are very happy about something, you might be _____.   joyful / helpful
8. If you plug in a cord, you _____ the cord.   connect / confess

☐ Correct

LESSON 17

A. New Words. Say each sound. Say each word.

1. <u>ph</u>one   <u>qu</u>est   <u>ph</u>ase
2. <u>qu</u>iz   ma<u>th</u>   <u>wr</u>ing
3. <u>ph</u>rase   <u>qu</u>ake   <u>qu</u>ote
4. <u>qu</u>ite   <u>wr</u>ite   <u>kn</u>it
5. Paul's quest for fun never seems to end.
6. Be careful when you wring out your socks.
7. Tell me how to write a phrase.
8. Will you knit me some mittens for this winter?

B. Challenge Words. Say the words.

gopher   knapsack   quiver   orphan   shipwreck
1 2   1 2   1 2   1 2   1 2

knockout   banquet   wrinkle   emphasis   equipment
1 2   1 2   1 2   1 2 3   1 2 3

C. Word Parts. Say the words.

<u>com</u>plete   hand<u>le</u>

D. Words with Word Parts. Say the words.

1. <u>com</u>bine   <u>com</u>pass   <u>con</u>dense   <u>con</u>vict   <u>de</u>fine
2. artic<u>le</u>   bott<u>le</u>   ridd<u>le</u>   factor<u>y</u>   correct<u>ly</u>
3. examp<u>le</u>   <u>con</u>dition   <u>com</u>for<u>table</u>   <u>per</u>fec<u>tion</u>

E. Sight Words. Say the words.

sure   don't   care   even   two

were   should   about   put   others

F. Passages. Read each part of the story. Write the story part number under the picture that goes with each story part.

Phase One

Part 1

Trish sat in the launch seat. She checked all the knobs again to make sure they were
₁₇ set correctly. Then, with a smile for Philip, she pressed the red button. The machine
₃₂ made a loud sound, and Trish was no longer there.

₄₂ Philip was quite shaken. He felt a quiver run up and down his spine. He felt sure he
₆₀ would not see Trish again. "I should have stopped her," he said to himself sadly, "even
₇₆ if I had to sit on her to do it. What will I say to Quay?" he sighed.

₉₄ Then someone said, "What will you say to Quay about what?"

Part 2

₁₀₅ Philip spun around quickly to see who had spoken. "Trish!" he squeaked. "You came
₁₁₉ back! Or did you even leave?" He ran to the launch seat and hugged her with glee.

₁₃₆ "I am surprised you are still waiting," Trish said. "Let's go before Quay comes in and
₁₅₂ finds us. I sure have a lot to tell you." Trish shut the time machine off and put back
₁₇₁ Quay's notes and graphs.

₁₇₅ "What do you mean that you are surprised that I am still waiting?" Philip asked as they
₁₉₂ left the room. "You left and came back in a flash. There was hardly time for me to sit down."

Part 3

₂₁₂ Trish and Philip went into the game room. Trish looked puzzled. "Philip, I spent all
₂₂₇ day in the past. Are you trying to be funny?" They discussed the time, but each was
₂₄₄ sure about how long Trish had been missing.

₂₅₂ "I don't know how to explain it," Philip said. "I am not even sure I care to. Just tell me
₂₇₂ what happened to you."

₂₇₆ "When I hit the button, there was light all around me. Then I must have fainted.
₂₉₂ If my math is right, when I woke up, I was in the 1300s. I was sitting on the grass by a
₃₁₄ big barn. I stayed there awhile and then I looked around. I don't think people could see
₃₃₁ me because no one spoke to me. By the way, finding my knight is easier said than done.
₃₄₉ All I saw were shopkeepers. I hit the wrist button and came back."

₃₆₂

G. **Practice Activity 1.** Read each question. Look back at the story on page 69. Fill in each blank with the best word.

Part 1

1. Where did Trish sit?

    She sat in the _____ _____.

2. What did she press?

    She pressed a _____ _____.

3. What happened when Trish pressed the button?

    The machine made a loud _____, and Trish was no longer there.

Part 2

4. What did Philip do when Trish returned?

    He ran to the launch seat and _____ her.

5. How fast did Trish come back?

    She came back in a _____.

Part 3

6. How long did Trish say she had been in the past?

    She said she had been in the past all _____.

7. Where was Trish when she woke up?

    She was sitting on the grass by a big _____.

8. Why did Trish think that people could not see her?

    No one _____ to Trish.

☐ Correct

H. **Practice Activity 2.** Fill in each blank with the better word.

1. _____ is Tom's pet _____.   Digger / gopher

2. The _____ saw a _____ swimming in the sea.   dolphin / fisherman

3. The _____ was a surprise for the _____.   banquet / housekeeper

4. The _____ in 1916 happened right off the _____.   seacoast / shipwreck

5. The _____ put his _____ on his back.   knapsack / scoutmaster

6. Beth's _____ was _____ in ink.   assignment / handwritten

☐ Correct

I. **Practice Activity 3.** Fill in each blank with the better word.

1. Jan will finish her math quiz. Jan will _____ her quiz.   complete / combine

2. Pete will tell about his trip. He will _____ his trip.   define / describe

3. Janis will join the dots on the graph. She will _____ the dots.   convict / connect

4. Barb will stay in the classroom. She will _____ there.   remain / remake

5. The jar was filled with milk. The _____ was filled with milk.   handle / bottle

6. Pam has many dresses. She has _____ of dresses.   plenty / factory

7. Dan got the math problem right. He did it _____.   correctly / directly

8. The factory was very big. The factory was _____.   enormous / joyous

☐ Correct

LESSON 18

A. New Words. Say each new sound. Say each word.

1. <u>kn</u>ow   <u>p</u>hone   <u>wr</u>ench
2. <u>q</u>uit   <u>kn</u>ife   <u>wr</u>ung
3. <u>wr</u>ist   <u>th</u>ick   <u>q</u>uick
4. <u>kn</u>ew   s<u>ph</u>inx   <u>kn</u>elt
5. Did Jan know the locker combination?
6. Will you quit your night job?
7. Turn your wrist this way when you hit the ball.
8. Ed went on a trip to the Sphinx.

B. Challenge Words. Say the words.

su<u>l</u>phur   p<u>l</u>aywright   un<u>kn</u>own   <u>l</u>iquid   <u>kn</u>uckle
1 2   1 2   1 2   1 2   1 2

<u>ph</u>antom   <u>wr</u>iter   tran<u>q</u>uil   s<u>q</u>uirrel   so<u>ph</u>omore
1 2   1 2   1 2   1 2   1 2 3

C. Word Parts. Say the words.

<u>com</u>plete   hand<u>le</u>

D. Words with Word Parts. Say the words.

1. <u>com</u>mit   <u>in</u>volve   <u>ex</u>plore   <u>com</u>plain   <u>con</u>fine   <u>be</u>come
2. terrib<u>le</u>   safel<u>y</u>   dail<u>y</u>   read<u>able</u>   possib<u>le</u>   twent<u>y</u>
3. <u>com</u>pan<u>y</u>   <u>re</u>member   <u>com</u>bus<u>tion</u>   <u>con</u>tain<u>ing</u>

E. Sight Words. Say the words.

sure   only   again   hold   about

your   also   give   want   would

F. **Passages.** Read each part of the story. Write the story part number under the picture that goes with each story part.

Into the Unknown

Part 1

For days, all Trish spoke of was wanting to go into the past again. "If you only knew how tremendous it was, you would be begging to go!" she said to Philip. "You also must remember you told me you would go with me if I came back safely. I did! Start thinking about a time you would like to explore." Philip would still not commit himself.

At last one day, Philip said, "I give up. You win, but I have one condition to make. This will be the last trip we take without telling Quay. For all you know, there may be something important we are not doing, and your first safe return was just luck. Is it a deal?"

"OK," Trish said, "but let's go quickly."

Part 2

They went to the room that housed the time machine. They knocked first to make sure Quay was not in the room. When they went in, Trish asked Philip where he wanted the time machine to take them.

"We are going to see the Sphinx and check out her riddle," Philip said. Trish started to speak, but Philip said, "Wait. I know people say that the Sphinx was a phantom and that she was not real. As the story goes, she would ask people a riddle. If they did not answer it right, she killed them. First of all, if the Sphinx is real, she cannot kill us. Besides, all the time machine knows is what we tell it. If there was no real Sphinx, the machine should take us to the Sphinx carved in rock on the Nile River. It cannot hurt to try."

Part 3

Philip wrote "SPHINX" on the screen while Trish set the buttons on the panel. Then they put on the wristbands that would make them return. They sat in the launch seat; Philip hit the start button, and with a quick thrust they were off!

They woke up on the banks of the Nile. There was the Sphinx—carved in rock. It was cool and tranquil, and the Sphinx was a sight to behold. After a while, they knew it was time to return. Back in the time-machine room again, they turned the machine off. Then Philip said, "Keep me company while I tell Quay her machine works."

"Not me!" Trish said. "Telling Quay was your condition, not mine. Besides, it's going to be hard enough to explain to a robot that we just wanted to explore the past."

G. **Practice Activity 1.** Read each question. Look back at the story on page 73. Fill in each blank with the best word.

Part 1

1. What did Trish want to do?

   Trish wanted to go into the _____ again.

2. What did Philip insist on when he agreed to go into the past?

   Philip insisted that they tell _____ about the trip when they returned.

Part 2

3. Why did they knock before they went into the room with the time machine?

   They knocked first to make sure _____ was not in the room.

4. What did Philip want to see?

   Philip wanted to see the _____.

Part 3

5. What did Philip write on the screen?

   He wrote "_____" on the screen.

6. Where did they wake up?

   They woke up on the banks of the _____ River.

7. What was the Sphinx?

   The Sphinx was _____ _____ _____ .

8. What was Quay?

   Quay was a _____.

☐ Correct

H. Practice Activity 2. Read the story. Fill in the blank with the best word.

When the bike's wheel began to squeak, Liz knew that something was wrong. If she did not stop the bike, Liz knew she would have a wreck. Liz quickly steered her bike onto the grass. When the wheels hit the grass, Liz was quickly thrown off the bike. Liz was smart to make the wreck happen on the grass.

1. The bike's wheel began to _____.
   squeak   stop   quit

2. Liz knew that something was _____.
   wrist   wreck   wrong

3. Liz knew that she would have a _____.
   wreck   wrong   wrung

4. Liz steered the bike onto the _____.
   rose   path   grass

5. Liz was thrown off her _____.
   wheel   bike   ground

6. Liz was smart to have the wreck happen on the _____.
   phone   grass   road

☐ Correct

I. Practice Activity 3. Underline the endings that make sense.

1. Philip can _____.
   a. put liquid into the pitcher
   b. wipe off the water from his windows
   c. slip through a knothole in the wall
   d. read a pamphlet about growing plants

2. Lewis could _____.
   a. put a jackknife in his knapsack
   b. get into a knapsack
   c. see a dolphin in the sea
   d. run quickly through quicksand

☐ Correct   ☐ Checking Up

LESSON 19

■ **New Sounds.** Say the words.

ma<u>tch</u>   bri<u>dge</u>

A. New Words. Say each sound. Say each word.

1. do<u>dge</u>   ca<u>tch</u>   e<u>dge</u>
2. ske<u>tch</u>   ju<u>dge</u>   sna<u>tch</u>
3. wi<u>tch</u>   <u>ch</u>ase   pa<u>tch</u>
4. i<u>tch</u>   lo<u>dge</u>   lo<u>ck</u>
5. Look out for the sharp edge of the table.
6. Tim will judge the art contest.
7. Pam put a patch on the tire that was leaking.
8. The bug bite on my hand is starting to itch.

B. Challenge Words. Say the words.

catcher	hodgepodge	pitcher	outstretch	hatchet
1 2	1 2	1 2	1 2	1 2
hitchhike	patchwork	kitchen	underneath	referee
1 2	1 2	1 2	1 2 3	1 2 3

C. Word Parts. Say the words.

<u>pro</u>vide   small<u>est</u>

D. Words with Word Parts. Say the words.

1. <u>pro</u>tect   <u>com</u>pass   <u>in</u>stant   <u>ex</u>plain   <u>con</u>trol   <u>pro</u>mote
2. need<u>le</u>   low<u>est</u>   posi<u>tion</u>   quick<u>ly</u>   sweet<u>est</u>   part<u>y</u>
3. <u>dis</u>cove<u>ry</u>   <u>pro</u>tec<u>tion</u>   <u>con</u>trap<u>tion</u>   <u>pro</u>duc<u>tion</u>

E. Sight Words. Say the words.

only   most   does   again   sure   four

also   many   some   walk   another   hour

F. Passages. Read each part of the story. Write the story part number under the picture that goes with each story part.

Baseball

Part 1

At one time or another, most boys and girls play baseball when they are growing up. Sometimes children play baseball at school, or they form teams to play after school or on weekends. People who like the game a lot can even watch baseball games on TV. Some boys grow up hoping to become a player on a team like the Cubs, the Mets, or the Dodgers. Players on these teams are paid to play baseball. Only the very best players are on these teams. The teams play each other to see which team is best.

Part 2

It takes a lot of skill and hard work to become an expert baseball player. Players must judge when to try to hit the ball that the pitcher throws. If the batter misses three times, the player is "out."

If a batter does not hit the ball, the catcher has to catch the pitched ball. This is a harder task than it may seem. Some pitchers throw the ball so fast that it may travel close to one hundred miles per hour. A catcher wears thick chest pads and a mask for protection.

Part 3

The object of a baseball game is to get as many "runs" as possible. A run is scored by a player running around the bases and crossing home plate. When a player hits a ball, the players from the other team chase and catch the ball. If a player hits the ball out of the ballpark, it is called a *home run*. If a ball hits the ground before a player can catch it, the batter runs to first base.

A batter may also get to first base by getting a "walk." This means the pitcher threw four balls that were out of reach for the batter. A pitcher who does not have good control of the ball can get his team into a jam quickly by walking too many players around the bases.

Baseball is fun to watch and fun to play. There are also other ways to enjoy baseball, as you will see.

G. **Practice Activity 1.** Read each question. Look back at the story on page 77. Fill in each blank with the best word.

Part 1

1. What sport do most boys and girls play at one time or another?

    Most boys and girls play _____ at one time or another.

2. What do some boys hope to be?

    Some boys hope to become a _____ on a team.

Part 2

3. What does it take to become a baseball player on a team?

    It takes a lot of _____ and hard _____.

4. What happens if the batter misses the ball three times?

    The batter is _____.

5. Why is it hard for the catcher to catch some balls?

    Some balls travel close to _____ _____ miles per hour.

6. How is the catcher protected?

    The catcher wears thick chest pads and a _____.

Part 3

7. What is the object of a baseball game?

    The object is to get as many _____ as possible.

8. How can a batter get a "walk"?

    If the pitcher throws _____ balls that are out of the batter's reach, the batter gets a "walk."

☐ Correct

H. **Practice Activity 2.** Read the story. Fill in each blank with the best word.

On a hot summer day, Jean went to the marsh to explore. As she stood next to the pond, a squeaking sound rose from the thick cattails. Without making a sound, Jean knelt down on the moist ground. Slowly she crept through the cattails on her knees. In front of Jean was a nest filled with five little wrens. Still on her knees, Jean crawled away from the wren nest.

1. Jean went to the marsh to _____.
   explore   squeak   creep

2. A squeaking sound rose from the _____.
   ground   pond   cattails

3. Jean knelt down on the moist _____.
   ground   cattails   path

4. She crept through the cattails on her _____.
   wrist   arms   knees

5. The nest was filled with five little _____.
   wrongs   wrecks   wrens

6. Jean crawled away on her _____.
   knees   legs   hands

☐ Correct

I. **Practice Activity 3.** Fill in each blank with the better word.

1. Miss Sanchez will give the children paper. She will _____ the paper.
   provide
   protect

2. Carla finished the task quickly. Carla worked _____.
   rapidly
   slowly

3. Robin will tell us the details of the plan. He will _____ the plan.
   explain
   explode

4. We will think about the plan. We will _____ the plan.
   control
   consider

5. The red berry was very sweet. It was the _____ berry in the bunch.
   sweetest
   smallest

6. Last night Jean unloaded the truck. The truck is _____.
   empty
   lucky

☐ Correct

LESSON 20

A. New Words. Say each sound. Say each word.

1. ri<u>dge</u> pi<u>tch</u> <u>ph</u>one
2. <u>k</u>now gru<u>dge</u> <u>qu</u>ote
3. fu<u>dge</u> ha<u>tch</u> ba<u>dge</u>
4. ma<u>tch</u> we<u>dge</u> pa<u>th</u>
5. Our ranch is just over the ridge.
6. I gave up my grudge when he said that he was sorry.
7. How many eggs do you think will hatch?
8. Do these green socks match my pants?

B. Challenge Words. Say the words.

hatchback pitchfork misjudge phonics
1 2   1 2   1 2   1 2

bamboo   coastline   authentic autograph
1 2   1 2   1 2 3   1 2 3

C. Word Parts. Say the words.

<u>pro</u>vide small<u>est</u>

D. Words with Word Parts. Say the words.

1. <u>pro</u>gram <u>un</u>known <u>re</u>tail <u>pro</u>file <u>ex</u>claim <u>de</u>crease
2. long<u>est</u> aw<u>ful</u> sad<u>dle</u> selec<u>tion</u> fast<u>est</u> gent<u>ly</u>
3. <u>con</u>struc<u>tion</u> <u>con</u>sider<u>able</u> <u>pro</u>pel<u>ler</u> forget<u>ful</u><u>ness</u>

E. Sight Words. Say the words.

even   does   most   only   again
through their   many   also   about

F. **Passages.** Read each part of the story. Write the story part number under the picture that goes with each story part.

Collectors

Part 1

    Many people think of baseball as a game or a hobby. For thousands of people, on the
17   other hand, baseball is a job. While some people play baseball as a job, others *sell* to
34   fans things that are related to baseball. Fans will pay a lot for baseball bats, caps, mitts,
51   shirts, and pants. A baseball with the autograph of an important player can be sold for
67   a lot to a baseball collector. Baseball programs with autographs also sell well.
80   The fastest growing hobby related to baseball is collecting baseball cards. This is no
94   longer just a hobby for children—for many people, it is their life's work.

Part 2

108   Baseball-card collectors have to know a great deal about the game and all the
122   players. They keep track of all this information through baseball-card newsletters and
134   by talking to other collectors. They can do this on the phone or at meetings.
149   Some cards cost more than others. A baseball card that is printed with a mistake on
165   it, for example, is prized by collectors. All the collectors want to get one. When the
181   baseball-card company fixes the mistake, there will not be many like that card. A slight
196   ridge on a card, on the other hand, makes the card less important than other cards.
212   Collectors also keep track of which players are hitting, batting, or catching well.
225   Their baseball cards cost much more than those of unknown players.

Part 3

236   There is a lot of information about a player or a team on a baseball card. The card
254   shows a player and which team he plays with. It also has his position on the team, how
272   well he bats or pitches, and any other teams he may have played for. Each card also
289   has a number because it is part of a complete set of baseball cards.
303   Some companies make only baseball cards. The hobby is growing so quickly that a
317   considerable number of new companies have started to print baseball cards also.
329

  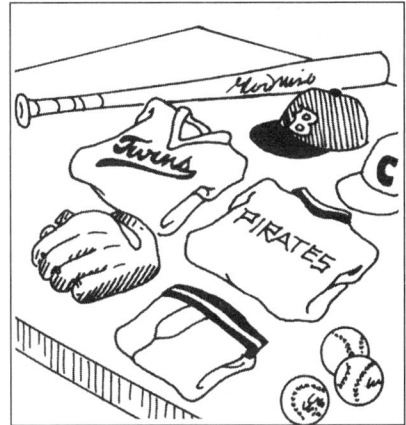

G. Practice Activity 1. Read each question. Look back at the story on page 81. Fill in each blank with the best word.

Part 1

1. What is the fastest growing hobby related to baseball?

   The fastest growing hobby related to baseball is _____ _____ _____.

2. Why do people collect baseball cards?

   People collect baseball cards as a hobby or their life's _____.

Part 2

3. How do baseball-card collectors get information about baseball?

   They read baseball-card _____ and talk to other _____.

4. Why is a baseball card with a mistake prized by collectors?

   There will not be many cards like that _____.

Part 3

5. What information is on a baseball card?

   A baseball card shows the player and tells which _____ he plays with.

6. What other information is on a baseball card?

   The card tells the player's _____ on the team and how well he _____ or pitches.

7. Why does a baseball card have a number on it?

   The number shows that the card is part of a _____ set of baseball cards.

8. Why would a new company want to make baseball cards?

   A new company might want to make baseball cards because the hobby is _____ so quickly.

☐ Correct

H. **Practice Activity 2.** Fill in each blank with the better word.

1. People should not _____ on the _____.
   hitchhike
   highway

2. There was a _____ at the _____ game.
   referee
   basketball

3. The waitress put the plates _____ the _____.
   underneath
   counter

4. The _____ was right off the _____.
   coastline
   shipwreck

5. The _____ told how to make a _____ quilt.
   patchwork
   pamphlet

6. The _____ was for the _____ player.
   saxophone
   applause

☐ Correct

I. **Practice Activity 3.** Fill in each blank with the better word.

1. We saw a TV show. We saw a TV _____.
   program
   provide

2. I do not know that girl. That girl is _____ to me.
   unwrap
   unknown

3. Jeff is very short. He is the _____ boy in the class.
   longest
   shortest

4. Mr. Martin will send three children to another room. The number of children in our classroom will _____.
   decrease
   describe

5. Molly was very ill. Molly felt _____.
   useful
   awful

6. The green scooter was very fast. It was the _____ scooter on the road.
   fastest
   slowest

7. The yellow candle was very small. It was the _____ candle on the birthday cake.
   smallest
   sweetest

8. Mark wrote a paper without a mistake. He wrote the paper _____.
   suddenly
   correctly

☐ Correct

83

LESSON 21

A. **New Words.** Say each sound. Say each word.

1. hi<u>tch</u>   bri<u>dge</u>   swi<u>tch</u>
2. ma<u>th</u>   nu<u>dge</u>   Mi<u>tch</u>
3. di<u>tch</u>   blo<u>tch</u>   bu<u>dge</u>
4. scra<u>tch</u>   swi<u>sh</u>   la<u>tch</u>
5. Switch seats with me, please.
6. Will you nudge Ned so he will wake up?
7. I can't get this blotch of paint out of my pants.
8. Release the latch so the dogs can go out.

B. **Challenge Words.** Say the words.

pitchfork	drawbridge	stretcher	hopscotch
1 2	1 2	1 2	1 2

switchover	graphite	gopher	yard line
1 2 3	1 2	1 2	1 2

C. **Word Parts.** Say the words.

<u>pro</u>vide   small<u>est</u>

D. **Words with Word Parts.** Say the words.

1. <u>pro</u>claim   <u>dis</u>cuss   <u>re</u>quire   <u>con</u>fuse   <u>com</u>bat   <u>pro</u>found
2. sharp<u>est</u>   sett<u>le</u>   mean<u>ness</u>   saf<u>est</u>   close<u>ly</u>   sta<u>tion</u>
3. <u>con</u>tain<u>er</u>   <u>for</u>ma<u>tion</u>   <u>re</u>jec<u>tion</u>   play<u>ful</u><u>ness</u>   <u>pro</u>gres<u>sion</u>

E. **Sight Words.** Say the words.

their   only   most   even   does

many   also   find   some   over

F. Passages. Read each part of the story. Write the story part number under the picture that goes with each story part.

Baseball Cards

Part 1

Boys and girls have been collecting baseball cards for a long time. Sometimes when you get a pack of baseball cards, there are five different cards and a stick of bubble gum. Many people like to collect cards of the players they like best. Some collectors try to get cards for a whole team. Still others get all the cards for all the baseball players. A set of all the players has close to 800 cards in it!

What can you do if you get more than one card for the same player? You can sell it or trade it to another collector who needs that card. In baseball-card clubs, collectors meet to sell, discuss, and trade cards. At these meetings, you may find old baseball cards that cost a lot.

Part 2

Many old baseball cards are quite hard to find. Collectors may have discarded the cards when the cards got old. Other collectors simply may have lost interest in collecting cards and discarded their collections. Because old cards were thrown out, there are not too many of them left. If you had some of these old baseball cards, you could become quite rich very fast. There is just one hitch—the card must be in mint (like new) condition. A scratch, a bent corner, or a printing blotch or smudge decreases how much a card is worth. Collectors carefully inspect and judge the condition of old cards.

Part 3

If your mom and dad collected baseball cards when they were children, you might see if you can find those cards. Look in old boxes or containers stored in the attic. This may mean some digging, but it could also make you rich.

There are some remarkable cards to look for. A 1963 Pete Rose baseball card sells for about $450. He played first base. You could also get $450 if you own a 1953 Willie Mays card. He was known for his hitting and base-stealing. Ty Cobb had more hits than any other man in baseball (4,191). His 1911 baseball card fetches about $500. Babe Ruth, a left-handed New York player, was best known for hitting home runs. His 1911 baseball card sells for $750. Last, but not least, there was a man named Honus Wagner, who played between 1909 and 1911 as a shortstop. *His* baseball card, of which there are not many, sells for over $20,000!

G. Practice Activity 1. Read each question. Look back at the story on page 85. Fill in each blank with the best word or number.

Part 1

1. How many baseball cards do you get in a pack?

   Often the pack will have _____ cards.

2. What can you do if you have more than one card for the same player?

   You can _____ or _____ the card to another collector.

3. Where might you meet other baseball-card collectors?

   You might meet them at a meeting of a baseball-card _____.

Part 2

4. What kind of condition do old cards need to be in?

   The cards need to be in _____ (like new) condition.

5. What would make a card not in mint condition?

   A card would not be in mint condition if it had a _____ or a

   _____ corner.

Part 3

6. What does a Pete Rose baseball card sell for?

   A Pete Rose baseball card sells for about _____.

7. What was Willie Mays known for?

   Willie Mays was known for his _____ and for

   _____ bases.

8. What was Babe Ruth best known for?

   He was known for hitting _____ _____.

☐ Correct

H. Practice Activity 2. Read each list. Cross out the word that does not belong in each list.

1. kitchen
   farmhouse
   bedroom
   bathroom

2. catcher
   hopscotch
   baseball
   pitcher

3. sludge
   mud
   grass
   muck

4. coastline
   shipwreck
   harbor
   knapsack

5. pocketknife
   jackknife
   hatchet
   penknife

6. dolphin
   sister
   orphan
   salesperson

7. gopher
   badger
   baboon
   bamboo

8. playground
   hopscotch
   soccer
   baseball

9. hammer
   gopher
   ruler
   spade

☐ Correct

I. Practice Activity 3. Fill in each blank with the better word.

1. If something needs to be fixed, then you could _____ it.   repair / remain

2. If we talk about a topic, we _____ the topic.   discuss / disown

3. If a car goes very fast, it might be the _____ car.   fastest / sharpest

4. If people come to a new land to stay, they _____ in the new land.   handle / settle

5. If a person is very mean, he might be known for his _____.   meanness / darkness

6. If a car was very fast, it would pass us _____.   closely / quickly

7. If you wanted to take a train ride, you would go to the train _____.   station / selection

8. If a rope was very long, it might be the _____ rope.   longest / safest

☐ Correct   ☐ Checking Up

87

LESSON 22

■ **New Sound.** Say the words.

c̲ell   peac̲e

A. **New Words.** Say each sound. Say each word.

1. c̲ell   glanc̲e   stic̲k
2. c̲one   voic̲e   twic̲e
3. c̲lip   spac̲e   tric̲k
4. peac̲e   c̲ame   c̲ent
5. Mark will glance out the window during class.
6. I brush my teeth at least twice a day.
7. Would you rather explore space or the deep sea?
8. You need peace and quiet when you work.

B. **Challenge Words.** Say the words.

circus   canteen   blockade   cinder
 1 2   1 2   1 2   1 2

absence   spacecraft   second   electric
 1 2   1 2   1 2   1 2 3

C. **Word Parts.** Say the words.

a̲bout   mo̲ment

D. **Words with Word Parts.** Say the words.

1. a̲gree   co̲mpound   pro̲fess   a̲void   co̲nsent   e̲xhibit
2. state̲ment hottes̲t   murderou̲s tab̲le   affec̲tion   governme̲nt
3. e̲xploration a̲mazement reflec̲tion dispos̲able profes̲sion unspeak̲able

E. **Sight Words.** Say the words.

every   their   does   only   sure
told   find   your   talk   again

F. **Passages.** Read each part of the story. Write the story part number under the picture that goes with each story part.

Lack of Funds

Part 1

Kay was walking home from school. As she drew close to an old oak tree, a voice said, "Stop! I come from outer space. If you want to see what a spaceman looks like, pick up that stick on the ground and tap the tree trunk twice. Do not be afraid. I come in peace."

"Joseph," Kay said, "you fooled me with that trick yesterday. Come out from your hiding place." She glanced around and saw Joseph walking in her direction.

"I should have known it would not work a second time," Joseph admitted. "It sure was fun when we saw the exciting space exhibit at the circus last week. I wish we could go again."

Part 2

"I agree," Kay said. "I would like to go, too, but I don't see how I can. I spent every last cent I had last week. It cost me fifty cents every time you made me go see the space exhibit. Between that and the admission price, not to mention all the snacks, I am flat broke. I am going to have to wait until the next time the circus comes before I can go again."

"I know what you mean," Joseph said. "My mom gave me a stern look when I asked her about it last night. On the other hand, she did not say no, so there may still be a chance. I will talk to her about it again and I will let you know what she says."

Part 3

Joseph got to the house before his mom came home. He quickly set the table—he hoped that would make his mom happy. Then he went to his room to start his homework.

Later, as Joseph and his mom were eating dinner, he asked her if he could go to the circus again. "Joseph," she said, "you have my consent. That's no problem, but you must pay your own way. Last week you made the choice to spend all I gave you in one night at the circus. If you want to go again, you will have to find a way to pay for it yourself. The circus will be around for another two weeks. If you put your mind to the task, I am sure you will think of something."

"OK, Mom, I will," he said. "I will talk to Kay and we will form a plan. See you later."

G. **Practice Activity 1.** Read each question. Look back at the story on page 89. Fill in each blank with the best word.

Part 1

1. What did the voice tell Kay to do?

    The voice told Kay to tap the tree _____.

2. Who did the voice belong to?

    The voice belonged to _____.

3. What did Joseph want to see again?

    Joseph wanted to see the _____ exhibit at the circus.

Part 2

4. Why was Kay unable to go to the circus again?

    Kay had spent every last _____ she had last week.

5. How much did it cost to see the exciting space exhibit?

    It cost _____ cents to see the exciting space exhibit.

Part 3

6. What did Joseph do before his mother got home?

    Joseph set the _____ and started his _____.

7. What did Joseph's mother say when he asked to go to the circus again?

    She said that he could go, but he would have to _____ for it himself.

8. How long would the circus be around?

    The circus would be around for another _____ _____.

☐ Correct

H. **Practice Activity 2.** Fill in each blank with the best word.

cents   twice   voice   cone   space   glanced   peace   sticks

1. Josh ate an ice-cream _____.
2. Tom's _____ was very loud.
3. The rocket ship blasted off into _____.
4. A stick of gum costs three _____.
5. If you do something two times, you do it _____.
6. Josh put ten more _____ on the fire.
7. If we do not fight, we can have _____.
8. Tom _____ up from his work when a truck went by.

☐ Correct

I. **Practice Activity 3.** Read each list. Cross out the word or word pair that does not belong in each list.

1. alphabet
   illustration
   portrait
   drawing

2. newspaper
   newsstand
   New York
   newsperson

3. toothbrush
   teaspoon
   shampoo
   toothpaste

4. outstanding
   disposable
   fantastic
   terrific

5. classmates
   schoolroom
   spacecraft
   classroom

6. thousand
   seventeen
   hundred
   scarce

7. canteen
   liquid
   trousers
   coffee

8. rocket
   spacecraft
   stretcher
   launch pad

9. gopher
   table
   squirrel
   raccoon

☐ Correct

LESSON 23

A. **New Words.** Say each sound. Say each word.

1. for<u>c</u>e   mi<u>c</u>e   <u>c</u>ause
2. <u>c</u>inch   pla<u>c</u>e   <u>c</u>row
3. sin<u>c</u>e   <u>c</u>ape   fen<u>c</u>e
4. <u>c</u>ease   <u>c</u>rawl   pri<u>c</u>e
5. We let the mice live up in the loft in the hay.
6. Which place is yours?
7. Ron will paint the fence while Beth trims the bushes.
8. The price of gas will rise in the winter.

B. **Challenge Words.** Say the words.

cartwheel (1 2)   center (1 2)   embrace (1 2)   cedar (1 2)

pencil (1 2)   kneecap (1 2)   democrat (1 2 3)   committee (1 2 3)

C. **Word Parts.** Say the words.

<u>a</u>bout   mo<u>ment</u>

D. **Words with Word Parts.** Say the words.

1. <u>a</u>mount   <u>com</u>prise   <u>pro</u>long   <u>a</u>part   <u>re</u>write   <u>con</u>struct
2. enjoy<u>ment</u>   hope<u>ful</u>   pay<u>ment</u>   smart<u>ness</u>   perfect<u>ly</u>   histor<u>y</u>
3. <u>a</u>part<u>ment</u>   <u>de</u>pres<u>sion</u>   <u>com</u>peti<u>tion</u>   <u>de</u>part<u>ment</u>

E. **Sight Words.** Say the words.

heard   any   every   their   don't

talk   about   some   through   there

F. **Passages.** Read each part of the story. Write the story part number under the picture that goes with each story part.

The Right Price

Part 1

    The next day after school, Joseph talked to Kay about ways to make some fast cash. "It's no cinch to get an after-school job," Joseph said. "Besides, I might not get paid until after the circus has left. Do you know any place that needs a good worker and that also pays a high amount?"

    "Well, that leaves out selling newspapers on a street corner," Kay said with a grin. "Shall we also scratch painting fences and digging ditches?" she teased. "OK, since you asked, there is one thing you seem to have overlooked. It was in the school newspaper. Don't you remember?"

Part 2

    Joseph paused for a second and then said, "I have not seen the newspaper yet. What are you talking about?"

    Kay reached for the newspaper. "Look," she said. "It says that the payment for handing out circus advertisements is a free ticket. For every two hundred ads you pass out, you get one free ticket. We could each do it and then we would get a ticket. I'm willing if you are. What do you say?"

    "Two hundred houses is a lot of walking," Joseph complained. "We better go pick up the advertisements if we are going to go through with this." As they were leaving, Joseph said, "What a brain I am! I have the perfect plan! Let's go get the advertisements."

Part 3

    On the way to get the circus advertisements, Joseph explained his plan. "We don't have to go to two hundred different *houses*," he said. "We only have to get them to two hundred different *people*. We can pass them out at those big apartment complexes on Cedar Street. It will hardly take any time at all, but it counts just the same," he said.

    The next night, Kay and Joseph went to the circus again. They enjoyed seeing the horses prance around the ring and the other shows. They stopped for a moment by the space exhibit, but they did not go in. "Maybe next time," Kay said to Joseph as they left. "At least we got to come again, and the price was right!"

G. **Practice Activity 1.** Read each question. Look back at the story on page 93. Fill in each blank with the best word.

Part 1

1. What did Joseph want to get in order to earn some money?

    He wanted to get an after-school _____ to earn some money.

2. Where did Joseph forget to look for a job?

    Joseph forgot to look in the school _____.

Part 2

3. What kind of job did the school newspaper tell about?

    It told about a job handing out _____ _____.

4. How many advertisements did Joseph need to hand out in order to get a ticket to the circus?

    He needed to hand out _____ _____ advertisements.

Part 3

5. Whom did Kay and Joseph have to give the advertisements to?

    Kay and Joseph had to give the advertisements to two hundred different _____.

6. Where did Joseph plan to hand out the advertisements?

    He planned to hand them out at the big _____ _____ on Cedar Street.

7. What did Kay and Joseph do the next night?

    They went to the _____ again.

8. What did Kay say about the price of their circus tickets?

    She said that the price was _____.

☐ Correct

H. Practice Activity 2. Read the story. Fill in each blank with the best word.

Cicero the Mouse said with a squeak, "Since it's dark, let's go to the barn. Maybe we can snatch some of Big Black's grain."

In a flash, the mice were off. They scampered over the bridge and down a path next to the fence. In an hour, they came to an open space. There stood the barn! Cicero did a cartwheel.

Inside the barn, the mice ran to the last stall. There they saw a bag of grain next to a pitchfork. In a second, the mice were eating the crunchy grain.

1. Where did Cicero want to go? Cicero wanted to go to the _____.

   bridge   barn   fence

2. What did he want to snatch? He wanted to snatch some of Big Black's _____.

   water   grain   hay

3. Where was the path? The path was next to the _____.

   fence   space   bar

4. What did Cicero do when he saw the barn? Cicero did a _____.

   bow   cartwheel   jump

5. Where in the barn did the mice find the bag of grain? The mice found the bag of grain in the _____.

   hay   place   stall

6. What was next to the bag of grain? A _____ was next to the bag of grain.

   somcone   pitchfork   stall

☐ Correct

I. Practice Activity 3. Read each list. Cross out the word or word pair that does not belong in each list.

1. cartwheel
   somersault
   hopscotch
   committee

2. oak
   cedar
   coleslaw
   bamboo

4. pencil
   autograph
   democrat
   handwritten

5. hammer
   sawmill
   screwdriver
   wrench

7. portrait
   drawing
   embrace
   sketch pad

8. newsstand
   spaceman
   fisherman
   storekeeper

☐ Correct

95

LESSON 24

A. **New Words.** Say each sound. Say each word.

1. pran<u>c</u>e   <u>c</u>urb   <u>c</u>ouch
2. <u>c</u>liff   <u>c</u>ents   prin<u>c</u>e
3. choi<u>c</u>e   <u>c</u>rew   la<u>c</u>e
4. <u>c</u>ool   ni<u>c</u>e   Ri<u>c</u>k
5. Make your horse prance through this part of the trail.
6. I am the prince in this year's play.
7. Do you like the white lace or the yellow lace?
8. She is such a nice person.

B. **Challenge Words.** Say the words.

citrus   faucet   playwright   census
1 2   1 2   1 2   1 2

boycott   cloister   civil   countess
1 2   1 2   1 2   1 2

C. **Word Parts.** Say the words.

<u>a</u>bout   mo<u>ment</u>

D. **Words with Word Parts.** Say the words.

1. <u>a</u>sleep   <u>re</u>spect   <u>pro</u>tons   <u>a</u>mong   <u>con</u>cern   <u>ex</u>pect
2. enjoy<u>ment</u>   shape<u>less</u>   men<u>tion</u>   entertain<u>ment</u>   part<u>ly</u>   memor<u>y</u>
3. <u>in</u>struc<u>tion</u>   <u>com</u>mit<u>ment</u>   <u>re</u>fresh<u>ment</u>   glamor<u>ous</u><u>ly</u>   <u>a</u>muse<u>ment</u>

E. **Sight Words.** Say the words.

any   every   their   don't   only

one   kind   another   from   walk

F. Passages. Read each part of the story. Write the story part number under the picture that goes with each story part.

First Snow

Part 1

    It had been snowing off and on for three days. Rick was looking out the window. The snow at the curb was close to two feet high. "Mom," he called, "may I go out and play? I want to make a snowman. All the kids have one in their yards—all except me," he said.

    His mom smiled, "Can't you think of some kind of entertainment that will keep you dry? I am concerned that you may catch another cold." She looked at Rick's pleading face. "OK, you may go out as long as you put on your hat, coat, boots, and mittens. Oh, grab a scarf, too."

    Rick ran to get his things while his mom sat at her desk. "Have a nice time," she said as he went out.

Part 2

    Outside, Rick began to pack the abundant snow into a big round ball. He looked up and down the street, but no one whom he knew was outside. He had no choice—he would have to make his snowman alone.

    A little while later, Rick went into the house to look for a hat for his snowman. As he came in, Prince wagged his tail and licked Rick's face. "Do you want to come out with me and play in the snow, Prince?" he asked the puppy. Prince wagged his tail faster. "Mom," Rick yelled, "Prince is going outside with me. Is that OK?"

    Rick's mom turned from the desk and said, "I don't think Prince will like the snow, Rick. He's still just a puppy, but you may try if you like."

Part 3

    Rick and Prince went out. Rick walked down the steps into the yard and called to Prince. Prince jumped down into a big snowdrift. He gave Rick a surprised look and then just stayed perfectly still. He lifted one paw and set it back down. Then he lifted another paw, but there was no dry place to put it. "Come on, Prince. Come here," Rick said.

    Prince began to slowly walk toward Rick. Each step seemed to be in slow motion. "Don't prance like a horse!" Rick giggled. "It's just snow!" As Prince came closer, Rick saw that Prince looked unhappy. "OK, pal," Rick said, "let's go back in. We can try this another day." Rick and Prince walked slowly back to the house.

_____   _____   _____

G. Practice Activity 1. Read each question. Look back at the story on page 97. Fill in each blank with the best word.

Part 1

1. Why did Rick want to go outside?

    Rick wanted to make a _____.

2. Why didn't Mom want Rick to go outside at first?

    She didn't want Rick to catch another _____.

Part 2

3. Why did Rick have to make his snowman alone?

    He had to make the snowman alone because no one whom he knew was

    _____.

4. Why did Rick go back into the house?

    He went inside to get a _____ for his snowman.

5. Who wanted to play outside with Rick?

    _____, Rick's puppy, wanted to play outside.

Part 3

6. When Prince jumped down into the snowdrift, what kind of look did he give Rick?

    Prince gave Rick a _____ look.

7. How did Prince walk in the snow?

    Prince walked very slowly. Each step seemed to be in _____

    _____.

8. Why did Prince and Rick go back into the house?

    Prince did not like the snow. He looked very _____.

☐ Correct

H. Practice Activity 2. Read each list. Cross out the word that does not belong in each list.

1. frustrate
   embarrass
   disappoint
   understand

2. playwright
   faucet
   drainpipe
   sewer

3. hermit
   kneecap
   pauper
   orphan

4. alphabet
   knapsack
   canteen
   jackknife

5. citrus
   cartwheel
   cedar
   cactus

6. spaceman
   circus
   arcade
   playground

7. charcoal
   saxophone
   sulphur
   graphite

8. pencil
   countess
   marker
   paper

9. lightning
   circus
   thundercloud
   monsoon

☐ Correct

I. Practice Activity 3. Fill in each blank with the better word.

1. All of the children were _____ _____ for Mark.
   asleep
   except

2. Mom said, "Peg, wait a _____. I will finish this _____."
   moment
   quickly

3. There was a green bottle _____ the _____ red bottles.
   among
   twenty

4. The birthday _____ gave Jim lots of _____.
   enjoyment
   party

5. Linda has a very good _____. She can _____ lots of facts.
   memory
   remember

6. Tom and Barb could not _____. Their _____ went on all night.
   disagreement
   agree

7. The reporter has to _____ her _____ for the morning newspaper.
   article
   rewrite

8. The _____ book had _____ chapters.
   twenty
   history

☐ Correct   ☐ Checking Up

LESSON 25

■ **New Sound.** Say the words.

ca<u>g</u>e   ur<u>g</u>e

A. **New Words.** Say each sound. Say each word.

1. crin<u>g</u>e   ca<u>g</u>e   <u>g</u>ee
2. <u>g</u>ent   <u>g</u>lee   mer<u>g</u>e
3. <u>g</u>ust   pa<u>g</u>e   stran<u>g</u>e
4. chan<u>g</u>e   <u>g</u>ate   <u>g</u>ist
5. Gee! This batch of letters is wet.
6. Drive in the right lane if you want to merge.
7. The front page of a newspaper is exciting to read.
8. Put exact change into the slot.

B. **Challenge Words.** Say the words.

margin   gently   cabbage   percent
 1 2   1 2   1   2   1   2

teenage   sausage   German   grapevine
 1   2   1   2   1   2   1   2

C. **Word Parts.** Say the word.

redd<u>ish</u>

D. **Words with Word Parts.** Say the words.

1. <u>a</u>tomic   <u>de</u>tergent   <u>re</u>place   <u>be</u>side   <u>pre</u>vent   <u>in</u>crease
2. pun<u>ish</u>   success<u>ful</u>   embank<u>ment</u> home<u>less</u>   educa<u>tion</u>   pub<u>lish</u>
3. <u>re</u>pay<u>ment</u>   <u>re</u>cent<u>ly</u>   <u>dis</u>trac<u>tion</u>   <u>comp</u>lete<u>ness</u>

E. **Sight Words.** Say the words.

father   year   their   every   again

even   two   many   others   through

F. Passages. Read each part of the story. Write the story part number under the picture that goes with each story part.

A Lesson from Europe

Part 1

　　Even as a little girl, Jane Addams could not understand why some people had so much and others had so little. Jane was lucky. Her father was a very rich man and they lived in a nice big house. When Jane and her father rode down the street in their buggy in the 1860s, Jane would see children playing in the road. They did not have a yard or lawn where they could play, as she did. Jane asked her father why this was so.

　　"I know it's hard to understand, Jane," said her father. "It may seem strange, but some people just don't have as much as others. They work hard, but they are poor. They cannot afford houses like ours."

　　Seeing poor children disturbed Jane. She decided she wanted to make a change. When she grew up, she did just that.

Part 2

　　Jane's mother had passed away when Jane was just two. Six years later, her father wed another woman. Jane got a new stepmother and stepbrother all at the same time. Jane and her stepbrother, who was her age, became quite close over the years.

　　Not many women went to college in those days, but Jane Addams did. She wanted to become a doctor and help poor people. Jane completed her basic college education, but she did not become a doctor. She had terrible problems with her back. The doctors treated her, but she had to stay in bed for a long time and could not complete her advanced schooling. Although her dream of becoming a doctor was unobtainable, Jane Addams still wanted to help poor people in some way. She only had to decide how.

Part 3

　　When Addams was feeling better, she went to Europe for two years with her stepmother. When they returned, Addams knew for sure she could not go back to school again.

　　Jane Addams returned to Europe with a woman she knew well, Ellen Starr. While the two women were in Europe, they visited a settlement house. This was a place where homeless or hungry people could go for help. At last, Addams saw how she could help poor people.

　　Jane Addams and Ellen Starr discussed the settlement house they had seen in Europe. Starr said she would like to help Addams start a settlement house. They returned home and began to plan their own house, a place to help the poor.

G. **Practice Activity 1.** Read each question. Look back at the story on page 101. Fill in each blank with the best word.

Part 1

1. What could Jane Addams not understand as a little girl?

   She could not understand why some people had so _____ and others had so _____.

2. What disturbed Jane?

   It disturbed Jane to see _____ children who did not have a good place to play.

Part 2

3. What happened when Jane Addams was two years old?

   When Jane Addams was two years old, her _____ passed away.

4. What did Jane Addams want to become?

   Jane Addams wanted to become a _____ and help poor people.

5. Why didn't Jane Addams become a doctor?

   Jane Addams had terrible problems with her _____. She had to stay in bed and could not finish her advanced schooling.

Part 3

6. Who returned to Europe with Jane Addams and visited a settlement house?

   Jane returned to Europe and visited a settlement house with _____ _____.

7. Who could go to the settlement house for help?

   _____ or _____ people could go to the settlement house for help.

8. What did Jane Addams and Ellen Starr decide to do?

   They decided to start a _____ _____.

☐ Correct

H. **Practice Activity 2.** Read each question. Underline the best words for each question.

1. Which words name animals?
   gopher   baboon
   faucet   squirrel
   pencil   raccoon

2. Which words name people?
   sportsman   faucet
   center   spaceman
   fisherman   inventor

3. Which words name ways of travel?
   subway train circus
   pencil   scooter
   rocket   seaplane

4. Which words name something to do with school?
   pencil   sausage
   gaslight   classroom
   alphabet   homeroom

5. Which words name foods?
   cabbage   oysters
   margin   sausage
   coleslaw   percent

6. Which words name body parts?
   elbow   teeth
   kneecap   cabbage
   kitchen   cheekbone

7. Which words name tools?
   second   circus
   screwdriver   pitchfork
   hatchet   hammer

8. Which words name something to do with water?
   center   harbor
   faucet   seacoast
   drawbridge   countess

☐ Correct

I. **Practice Activity 3.** Fill in each blank with the better word.

1. The clay pot was red. It had a _____ glaze.

   reddish
   punish

2. Jim and Mark will wash the dishes. First, they will fill the sink with with water and _____.

   decrease
   detergent

3. Barb broke a dish. She will _____ the dish.

   replace
   remain

4. Mark put the dish on the shelf next to the plant.
   He put the dish _____ the plant.

   beside
   belong

5. The children go to school. They will get an _____ in school.

   education
   station

6. The number of children at th school will get larger this year.
   The number of children will _____.

   indeed
   increase

☐ Correct

103

LESSON 26

A. New Words. Say each sound. Say each word.

1. g<u>e</u>rm   sta<u>ge</u>   <u>ge</u>m
2. a<u>ge</u>   <u>g</u>lad   <u>u</u>r<u>ge</u>
3. lar<u>ge</u>   <u>g</u>oose   <u>g</u>rew
4. dr<u>ug</u>   <u>G</u>ene   spon<u>ge</u>
5. There is a rock-and-gem show in the city this week.
6. What is the age of your dog?
7. I would like a large serving of green beans, please.
8. Use a wet sponge to clean up that spill.

B. Challenge Words. Say the words.

ginger   disgust   target   sagebrush
1 2   1 2   1 2   1 2

greenhouse   stagecoach   Pacific   gingersnap
1 2   1 2   1 2 3   1 2 3

C. Word Parts. Say the word.

redd<u>ish</u>

D. Words with Word Parts. Say the words.

1. <u>ex</u>ercise   <u>con</u>firm   <u>com</u>plete   <u>a</u>greed   <u>pro</u>ceed   <u>a</u>lert
2. furn<u>ish</u>   wis<u>est</u>   tor<u>ment</u>   cir<u>cle</u>   atten<u>tion</u>   fin<u>ish</u>
3. <u>in</u>vest<u>ment</u>   help<u>less</u><u>ly</u>   <u>re</u>duc<u>tion</u>   <u>dis</u>respect<u>ful</u>

E. Sight Words. Say the words.

father   year   care   women   any

their   talk   over   other   also

F. **Passages.** Read each part of the story. Write the story part number under the picture that goes with each story part.

Hull House of Chicago

Part 1

When Jane Addams and Ellen Starr returned to Chicago, they rented a large old house called Hull House in a rundown part of Chicago. It was named Hull House because some people named Hull had owned it many years before. Addams and Starr then proceeded to clean, paint, and furnish the house. When they were finished, they urged poor people to come to Hull House for help.

During the day, the people who worked at Hull House cared for children whose fathers and mothers were at work. There were also clubs for school-age children to take part in after school. At night, there were concerts and plays for poor people to attend.

Hull House was a good start, but Jane Addams wanted to do more.

Part 2

Jane Addams discovered a lot about poor people and their lives. She knew that many changes had to be made so that their lives would be better.

Working conditions were terrible. Many children, like adults, worked long hard hours. Addams worked to get laws changed to limit children's working hours and to make working conditions better for all workers. She also knew that she could not make all the changes alone.

During the next stage of her life, Jane Addams began to take on bigger projects. For example, a huge concern of hers was that women could not vote. She joined with other women to try to get the voting laws changed.

Part 3

With the help of many other brave women, Jane Addams helped women get the right to vote in 1920. She also was the leader of the Women's Peace Party. This group wanted people to talk about their problems rather than fight.

At the same time, Hull House continued to expand. People from all over came to see Hull House. When these people returned home they began settlement houses like Hull House.

Jane Addams was also an author. She wrote *Twenty Years at Hull House*, which was published in 1910. Some years later, in 1931, the Nobel Peace Prize was bestowed upon Jane Addams. She had spent much of her life trying to make life better for many people.

G. **Practice Activity 1.** Read each question. Look back at the story on page 105. Fill in each blank with the best word or number.

Part 1

1. What did Jane Addams and Ellen Starr call their settlement house?

   They called it _____ _____.

2. What did the people at Hull House do during the day?

   They cared for _____ while their fathers and mothers went

   to _____.

Part 2

3. What laws concerning children did Jane Addams work to change?

   She worked to change laws to limit children's _____

   _____.

4. What laws concerning women did Jane Addams work to change?

   She worked to change laws so that women could _____.

Part 3

5. When did women get the right to vote?

   Women got the right to vote in _____.

6. What party was Jane Addams a leader of?

   She was a leader of the Women's _____ _____.

7. What book did Jane Addams write?

   She wrote _____ _____ at _____

   _____.

8. What prize did Jane Addams win for helping people?

   She won the _____ _____ _____.

☐ Correct

H. Practice Activity 2. Read each story. Underline the endings that make sense.

1. The jeweler had a large display case in his store. In the display case were _____.
   a. large jewels
   b. lace dresses
   c. strange gems

2. The children wrote a play for the school. Gene was to be a prince in the play. On the day of the play, Gene _____.
   a. changed into his prince cloak
   b. got a sponge at the drugstore
   c. pranced onto the stage

3. The prince likes to ride his horse in the summer. One day the prince _____.
   a. rode along the fence to the bridge
   b. put a sponge in the bathtub
   c. rode out to the ridge

4. Gene works in a drugstore. He stands at the counter all day. One day Gene _____.
   a. crawled under the fence
   b. sold a sponge to Pete
   c. gave change to Beth

☐ Correct

I. Practice Activity 3. Read each question. Underline the best words for each question.

1. Which words name fun places?
   arcade   dolphin
   amusement park circus
   absence   playground

2. Which words name people?
   teenager   democrats
   August   hitchhikers
   spacemen   catchers

3. Which words name numbers?
   seventeen thousand
   hundred   thirteen
   fifteen   center

4. Which words name things related to the sea?
   harbor   saddle
   cedar   seacoast
   sagebrush seashore

5. Which words name foods?
   gingersnaps radish
   sausage   cabbage
   stagecoach   gaslight

6. Which words name games?
   hopscotch   ginger
   finish   baseball
   basketball grapevines

7. Which words name plants?
   citrus trees sagebrush
   cartwheels   greenhouse
   oak trees   grapevines

8. Which words name ways to travel?
   stagecoach seaplane
   sailboat   rubbish
   scooter   subway

☐ Correct

107

LESSON 27

A. **New Words.** Say each sound. Say each word.

1. sur<u>ge</u>   <u>g</u>oose   <u>g</u>ist
2. <u>g</u>reen   pa<u>g</u>es   <u>g</u>ash
3. bul<u>ge</u>   <u>g</u>lee   ran<u>ge</u>
4. sta<u>ge</u>   mer<u>ge</u>   ran<u>g</u>er
5. There was a surge of lightning during the storm.
6. Tape the torn pages of your book.
7. Please remove the teapot from the top of the range.
8. Gail plans to be a ranger in the fall.

B. **Challenge Words.** Say the words.

drugstore   danger   gateway   carpool
 1 2   1 2   1 2   1 2

giraffe   urgent   congress   autograph
1 2   1 2   1 2   1 2 3

C. **Word Parts.** Say the word.

redd<u>ish</u>

D. **Words with Word Parts.** Say the words.

1. <u>a</u>fraid   <u>in</u>come   <u>ex</u>cellent   <u>pre</u>cede   <u>de</u>tect   <u>a</u>dopt
2. ship<u>ment</u>   rubb<u>ish</u>   thir<u>ty</u>   unc<u>le</u>   tarn<u>ish</u>   nic<u>est</u>
3. <u>in</u>stru<u>ment</u>   <u>ex</u>pres<u>sion</u>   <u>un</u><u>a</u>fraid   <u>in</u>correct<u>ly</u>

E. **Sight Words.** Say the words.

year   father   don't   give   does

many   hold   through   also   mind

F. Passages. Read each part of the story. Write the story part number under the picture that goes with each story part.

Dolphins

Part 1

Many people have seen dolphins on TV or in shows at amusement parks. They have seen dolphins leap out of the surging sea or a large pool. We know many things about dolphins, but we are still trying to discover more about them.

Some people think dolphins look like sharks because they are both gray, but there are many differences. For example, a shark's tail moves from side to side while a dolphin's tail moves up and down. Another big difference is the size of the brain. A shark's brain is quite little; a dolphin's brain is as big as that of a fully grown person.

Dolphins seem to be very smart. Many people would like to know how smart dolphins are.

Part 2

Dolphins like to play, so dolphin trainers teach them tricks that seem like play. When the dolphin performs a trick, like jumping high out of the water, the trainer gives the dolphin a treat as a reward. This is the way trainers teach dolphins. They give the dolphins fish to eat when they want the dolphins to continue an action. The dolphin soon knows what to do to get a fish. After a while, the dolphin becomes good at it and does it for fun as well as for fish. However, if a dolphin does not want to do a trick, it will not do it. Even a trainer cannot make a dolphin change its mind!

Part 3

There is another excellent way to teach dolphins—through the use of computers.

Dolphins talk to each other by making clicks and other sounds that travel through the water. Through the use of a computer, a trainer's voice can be changed into dolphin clicks and sounds. The trainer can then use the computer to talk to the dolphins and tell them what to do. The sound travels through the water to the dolphins.

Dolphins have an excellent sense of hearing. They can detect sound at a long range. If a trainer drops something small into the water that the dolphin cannot see, the dolphin can swim right to it.

One of the nicest things about dolphins is their gentleness. Sometimes a dolphin will even let a swimmer hold onto a fin and will give the swimmer a ride. Of course, the swimmer should be certain that it is a dolphin and not a shark!

G. **Practice Activity 1.** Read each question. Look back at the story on page 109. Fill in each blank with the best word.

Part 1

1. What way does a shark's tail move?

    A shark's tail moves from _____ to _____.

2. What way does a dolphin's tail move?

    A dolphin's tail moves _____ and _____.

3. How is the shark's brain different from the dolphin's brain?

    The shark's brain is quite _____, while the dolphin's brain is

    as _____ as that of a man or woman.

Part 2

4. What do dolphins like to do?

    They like to _____.

5. What do trainers do if they want the dolphins to continue an action?

    The trainers give the dolphins _____ to eat.

Part 3

6. How do dolphins talk to each other?

    Dolphins talk to each other by making _____ and other sounds.

7. How does the computer help the trainer talk to the dolphin?

    The computer changes the trainer's _____ into dolphin

    _____ and sounds.

8. What is one of the nicest things about dolphins?

    Dolphins are very _____.

☐ Correct

H. Practice Activity 2. Read each story. Underline the endings that make sense.

1. Liz and Trish are planning to put on a play for their class. On Thursday, Liz and Trish _____.
   a. got up on the stage
   b. changed into their costumes
   c. put a goose into a cage

2. The housekeeper likes to keep the house very clean. This morning, the housekeeper _____.
   a. turned the pages in her newspaper
   b. cleaned the sink with a sponge
   c. killed the germs in the toilet

3. Mr. Perez went to the drug store. At the store, Mr. Perez _____.
   a. put a large sponge in his cart
   b. went up on the stage
   c. chose a green scratch pad

4. Ms. Sanchez went to the jewelry store. At the jewelry store, the jeweler _____.
   a. showed her a large gem
   b. urged her to get a new necklace
   c. showed her a sponge

☐ Correct

I. Practice Activity 3. Fill in each blank with the best word.

| afraid | excellent | shipment | thirty |
| rubbish | uncle | detect | adopt |

1. Barb did not like the gusty wind, thunder, or lightning. She was _____.

2. I _____ a note of sadness. Is something wrong?

3. This summer, Mark's aunt and _____ will come to visit.

4. Fred and Chris plan to _____ a girl and a boy. They want two children.

5. The attic is filled with _____. We need to throw it all in the trash.

6. The store got a large _____ of toys.

7. Mark did the math page correctly. On top of his page, the teacher wrote "_____."

8. In September, there were twenty children in the class. By May, there were _____ children in the class.

☐ Correct   ☐ Checking Up

LESSON 28

■ **New Sound.** Say the words.

d<u>ow</u>n   cr<u>ow</u>d

A. **New Words.** Say each sound. Say each word.

1. <u>ow</u>l   bl<u>ow</u>n
2. fl<u>ow</u>n   pl<u>ow</u>
3. cl<u>ow</u>n   sh<u>ow</u>
4. d<u>ow</u>n   cr<u>ow</u>d
5. I saw a large owl at the zoo.
6. All the birds have flown south for the winter.
7. What time is the late show?
8. There was a large crowd at the fair.

B. **Challenge Words.** Say the words.

showtime	grown-up	owner	chowder
1 2	1 2	1 2	1 2
cowhand	crowbar	sundown	somehow
1 2	1 2	1 2	1 2

C. **Word Parts.** Say the word.

fin<u>al</u>

D. **Words with Word Parts.** Say the words.

1. <u>a</u>dore   <u>pro</u>claim   <u>con</u>dense   <u>de</u>mote   <u>ex</u>change   <u>be</u>have
2. norm<u>al</u>   furn<u>ish</u>   frank<u>ness</u>   gener<u>ous</u>   gent<u>le</u>   numer<u>al</u>
3. fin<u>al</u><u>ly</u>   <u>con</u>vers<u>ation</u>   natur<u>ally</u>   <u>pun</u><u>ish</u><u>ment</u>

E. **Sight Words.** Say the words.

| thought | friend | anyway | someone | somehow |
| were | sure | two | their | kind |

F. **Passages.** Read each part of the story. Write the story part number under the picture that goes with each story part.

Planning a Talent Show

Part 1

"This talent show is more work than I thought it would be," Penny said to Ted. "I thought all I would have to do is judge the acts on stage and proclaim the winner. Here I am trying to decide how many clown acts and singing cowboys we can use. I also have to talk Ms. Downs into printing the tickets for a low price and find someone to work the lights. I sure could use your assistance, Ted."

"I don't know exactly what I can do, Penny," Ted said, "but I will help any way I can. Ms. Downs is the owner of Showtime, the store on Page Street, right? If you want, I will have a conversation with her after school. Maybe I can convince her to print the tickets at a good price. After all, it is for a good cause."

Part 2

At Penny's house later, Ted said, "Well, the ticket problem is solved. At first, Ms. Downs turned me down. Finally, I explained that the talent show was to raise funds for the school band. Then she said she adored our plans and became quite generous. She agreed to print the tickets for free! Somehow I think it had something to do with the fact that her uncle conducts the band," he said grinning. "Anyway, what's next on the list?"

Penny looked down at her list. "We still need someone to sell the tickets, someone to show people to their seats, someone to work the lights, and a clean-up crew for after the show. Those are the main tasks," she said.

"I will talk to our friends at school," Ted said. "Between the two of us, we should be able to find people for all those jobs."

Part 3

The night of the talent show was approaching. Penny had decided to set a limit of two for each kind of act. As she explained to Ted, "We cannot have five clown acts. The crowd will simply not enjoy the show. There must be someone out there who can juggle or dance or something." Then Penny asked Ted how the ticket sales were going.

"It seems a little slow," Ted said, "but it's hard to tell. I think most of the people are waiting to get their tickets on the night of the show. You just keep working on the show itself. I am sure we will have a big crowd."

_____ _____ _____

G. **Practice Activity 1.** Read each question. Look back at the story on page 113. Fill in each blank with the best word.

Part 1

1. What is Penny planning?

    Penny is planning a _____ _____.

2. Who did Penny ask to help with the talent show?

    Penny asked _____ to help with the talent show.

3. What did Ted say that he would do?

    He said that he would talk with _____ _____ and

    try to convince her to print the _____ for a good price.

Part 2

4. Why did Ms. Downs decide to print the tickets for free?

    She decided to print the tickets for free because the talent show would raise funds

    for the _____ _____.

5. What did Penny need people to help her with?

    She needed someone to sell _____, someone to work the

    _____, a _____-_____ crew, and

    someone to show people to their _____.

6. Whom was Ted going to ask to help with the talent show?

    Ted was going to ask their _____ at school to help with the

    talent show.

Part 3

7. How many acts of each kind did Penny decide to have?

    She decided to set a limit of _____ for each kind of act.

8. When did Ted think people would get their tickets?

    He thought they would get their tickets on the _____ of the show.

☐ Correct

H. **Practice Activity 2.** Read each story. Underline the endings that make sense.

1. At the zoo, the crowd looked at many animals. The crowd saw _____.
   a. an owl in a cage
   b. a clown on a stage
   c. a baboon by a stream

2. At the circus, the crowd saw many things. They saw _____.
   a. a horse prance around the ring
   b. a farmer plow his crops
   c. a clown doing tricks

3. The farmer works hard on his farm. The farmer _____.
   a. plows the soil before he plants his crops
   b. cuts down the weeds that grow among his plants
   c. sees a clown at the circus

4. The clowns in the circus do many funny things. The clowns _____.
   a. show the crowd tricks
   b. read the pages of a newspaper
   c. dance and prance around the circus stage

☐ Correct

I. **Practice Activity 3.** Read each list. Cross out the word or word pair that does not belong in each list.

1. screwdriver
   crowbar
   chowder
   hammer

2. grown-up
   somehow
   teenager
   preschooler

3. sundown
   morning
   sunup
   engine

4. sundown
   cowhand
   jeweler
   salesperson

5. chowder
   gingersnaps
   cabbage
   grown-up

6. giraffe
   congress
   baboon
   raccoon

7. sausage
   gingersnaps
   hamburger
   committee

8. spaceman
   rocket
   launch pad
   showtime

9. stagecoach
   crowbar
   seaplane
   sailboat

☐ Correct

115

LESSON 29

A. **New Words.** Say each sound. Say each word.

1. fr<u>ow</u>n   br<u>ow</u>
2. gr<u>ow</u>l   sl<u>ow</u>
3. gr<u>ow</u>th   b<u>ow</u>l
4. sh<u>ow</u>n   br<u>ow</u>n
5. Her frown disappeared when she saw the teddy bear.
6. I am a slow driver.
7. The growth rate of the eagle is astonishing!
8. Your brown shoes look good with that outfit.

B. **Challenge Words.** Say the words.

snow·drift   down·stream   snow·plow   home·own·er

blow·torch   fel·low·ship   gun·pow·der   towns·man

C. **Word Parts.** Say the word.

fin<u>al</u>

D. **Words with Word Parts.** Say the words.

1. <u>p</u>revail   <u>e</u>xcuse   <u>a</u>wait   <u>d</u>istant   <u>c</u>ontinue   <u>a</u>larm
2. miner<u>al</u>   numer<u>ous</u>   catt<u>le</u>   swift<u>ly</u>   pig<u>ment</u>   sever<u>al</u>
3. <u>con</u>sumer   expres<u>sion</u>   expand<u>able</u>   informal<u>ly</u>

E. **Sight Words.** Say the words.

thought   someone   friend   only   any

their   care   over   sure   don't

F. **Passages.** Read each part of the story. Write the story part number under the picture that goes with each story part.

The Show Must Go On

Part 1

Ted and Penny were sitting in the dining room at Ted's house. They were discussing the final plans for tonight's talent show. "OK, Penny," Ted said, "let's go through your list again. You have been frowning for two days now. Relax, will you? We have things under control. I got my friends to agree to take care of all the things you said you needed. I wish I knew what you're so concerned about."

"It's hard to explain, Ted," Penny said. "I just have this feeling. Several things could go wrong, you know."

"It's silly to waste your time thinking about what might happen," Ted said. "If you keep this up, you will be the only one who will not enjoy the show. Let's go back to your list and check it again. That should help."

Part 2

Later that afternoon, Penny got a phone call at home. It was from Ms. Brown, the school nurse. "I am afraid I have some bad news for you, Penny," Ms. Brown said. "I cannot be one of the judges for the talent show tonight. My little boy is ill, and I don't want to leave him alone. I am sure you can find someone to take my place," she continued. Penny told her she would and thanked her for calling. Then she phoned Ted.

"Don't be alarmed," Ted said. "I will find someone. You just meet me at school around six as we agreed. I will bring the new judge with me."

Part 3

At 6:15 that night, Penny still had not seen Ted. She had a grim look on her face. Finally, she saw him walk in with a tall woman in a brown overcoat. "Penny," Ted said, "this is Ms. Downs from Showtime. She has agreed to fill in as a judge. Will you show her where the judge's table is?" he asked. Penny did, and then walked back to talk with Ted.

"Thanks for all your help, Ted. I should have known you would not let me down. The show will be starting soon. Let's go find our seats. From now on, you and I will be just part of the crowd. Let's enjoy the show." They walked to their seats. Penny was finally smiling.

G. **Practice Activity 1.** Read each question. Look back at the story on page 117. Fill in each blank with the best word.

Part 1

1. Who was upset about the talent show?

   _____ was upset about the talent show.

2. How did Ted know that Penny was upset and nervous about the show?

   He saw that Penny had been _____ for two days.

3. What did Ted say that they should do?

   He said that they should check Penny's _____ again.

Part 2

4. Who called Penny and said that she could not be a judge?

   _____ _____ said that she could not be a judge.

5. Who said he would find a new judge?

   _____ said he would find a new judge.

Part 3

6. Why did Penny have a grim look on her face at 6:15?

   Penny had not seen _____ and the new judge.

7. Who had agreed to fill in as a judge?

   _____ _____ had agreed to be a judge.

8. How do you know that Penny was happy when the show began?

   Penny was finally _____.

☐ Correct

H. Practice Activity 2. Read each list. Cross out the word or word pair that does not belong in each list.

1. cowhand
   storekeeper
   giraffe
   grown-up

2. snowdrift
   snowplow
   snowman
   showtime

3. sagebrush
   blowtorch
   cedar
   oak tree

4. crowbar
   blowtorch
   sundown
   hatchet

5. downstream
   townsman
   landowner
   homeowner

6. stagecoach
   tractor
   snowplow
   homeowner

7. rocket
   spaceman
   drugstore
   space ride

8. faucet
   sewer
   snowdrift
   drainpipe

9. wrist
   kneecap
   elbow
   gunpowder

☐ Correct

I. Practice Activity 3. Fill in each blank with the best word.

| final | excused | continued | cattle |
| alarm | swiftly | several | asleep |

1. On the ranch, the cowhands raise _____.
2. By 9:00, the children will be sound _____.
3. The train was very fast. It _____ passed the train station.
4. When the fire broke out, Jane pulled the fire _____.
5. When the children finished their dinner, they asked to be _____ from the table.
6. When the _____ bell rang, the children sat down.
7. _____ homeowners met at the town hall.
8. Jeff wanted to finish mowing the lawn. When the rain stopped, Jeff _____ to mow the lawn.

☐ Correct

LESSON 30

A. **New Words.** Say each sound. Say each word.

1. fl<u>ow</u>er   cr<u>ow</u>
2. cr<u>ow</u>n   t<u>ow</u>n
3. gr<u>ow</u>   p<u>ow</u>der
4. g<u>ow</u>n   gl<u>ow</u>
5. "Caw, caw," said the crow when it saw the piles of corn.
6. The queen is putting her crown on display this week.
7. Remember to get baby powder at the store.
8. The glow from the sun slowly faded as night approached.

B. **Challenge Words.** Say the words.

cow·hide (1 2)   row·boat (1 2)   night·gown (1 2)   pent·house (1 2)

out·grown (1 2)   sun·flow·er (1 2 3)   wid·ow·er (1 2 3)   marsh·mal·low (1 2 3)

C. **Word Parts.** Say the word.

fin<u>al</u>

D. **Words with Word Parts.** Say the words.

1. <u>pre</u>flight   <u>pro</u>pose   <u>a</u>mend   <u>de</u>rail   <u>ex</u>cite   <u>a</u>new
2. hospit<u>al</u>   pal<u>est</u>   func<u>tion</u>   strug<u>gle</u>   clear<u>ly</u>   ment<u>al</u>
3. <u>ex</u>cite<u>ment</u>   <u>un</u>usual   <u>pro</u>vi<u>sion</u>   <u>ex</u>act<u>ness</u>

E. **Sight Words.** Say the words.

friend   thought   almost   anyone   every

over   sure   told   another   even

F. Passages. Read each part of the story. Write the story part number under the picture that goes with each story part.

Wedding Weekend

Part 1

Gale and Bob were walking home from school. "What did you think of that math quiz today?" Gale asked.

"It was a struggle," Bob said, "but I think I did a good job. You know, Gale, I would rather take another test than go home right now."

Gale gave her friend a look of surprise. "Clearly you are ill," Gale said. "Let me feel your brow. Shall I take you directly to the hospital?" she joked. "You must admit that was an unusual statement. Let's go over to my house, and you can tell me all about it." They continued down the road to Gale's house.

Part 2

Gale and Bob went into the house and sat down in the den. Bob began to explain. "You forget, Gale. This is the wedding weekend at my house. When Todd proposed to my sister, Joan, I did not dream what a mess this wedding would turn into. I think my sister has invited the entire town. Our house is filled with flowers and people from out of town. All anyone talks about is wedding gowns or how the bride-to-be is glowing. My mother likes the excitement. I even think my father is enjoying it. I just want it to be over so my life can get back to normal. I even lost my bedroom to two of my uncles," he moaned.

Gale and Bob talked for a while. As Bob was leaving, Gale said, "Try to enjoy yourself. Who knows? It might be fun. See you soon."

Part 3

The next day was bright and clear. Bob had to admit that it was a nice day for a wedding. After he was dressed, he went to find Joan. Her room was filled with friends helping her get dressed. He sat down and watched her put on her powder and lipstick.

Finally, his sister saw him and said, "You look handsome, Bob. Are you all set?" Bob looked puzzled. Joan continued, "I am sure I told you that we want you to bring us our rings. You are an important part of this wedding. This is a big day for all of us. It's almost time to go." His sister gave him a big hug.

The wedding turned out to be nice for Bob after all.

G. **Practice Activity 1.** Read each question. Look back at the story on page 121. Fill in each blank with the best word.

Part 1

1. Where were Gale and Bob walking?

    They were walking _____ from _____.

2. What had happened in school that day?

    Gale and Bob had taken a _____ _____.

Part 2

3. Why didn't Bob want to go home?

    His sister's _____ was this weekend.

4. Who liked all of the wedding excitement?

    Bob's _____ liked the excitement.

5. Why did Bob want the wedding to be over?

    He wanted life to get back to _____.

Part 3

6. What did Bob do after he got dressed for the wedding?

    He went to find _____.

7. Who was helping Joan get dressed?

    Joan's _____ were helping her get dressed.

8. What did Bob get to do in the wedding?

    He got to bring the _____ to Joan and Todd.

☐ Correct

H. Practice Activity 2. Read each list. Cross out the word that does not belong in each list.

1. rowboat
   seaplane
   sagebrush
   stagecoach

2. townhouse
   penthouse
   nightgown
   apartment

3. jacket
   trousers
   sunflower
   nightgown

4. snowplow
   snowdrift
   showtime
   snowbank

5. widower
   penthouse
   landowner
   homeowner

6. cowhide
   stagecoach
   outgrown
   cowhand

7. grown-up
   teenager
   toddler
   sundown

8. sunflower
   rowboat
   sagebrush
   grapevine

9. marshmallow
   hamburger
   cowhide
   cabbage

☐ Correct

I. Practice Activity 3. Fill in each blank with the better word.

1. The girl was very pale. In fact, she was the _____ girl in the hospital.
       palest
       longest

2. When you are sick, you usually stay home. But if you are very sick, you might go to the _____.
       hospital
       unusual

3. Pam saw the owl in the distant trees. She could see the owl _____.
       gently
       clearly

4. Putting the toy train's track together was hard for Jeff. Jeff had to _____ to get the track together.
       struggle
       needle

5. The last train of the day left at 9:00. It was the _____ train of the day.
       normal
       final

6. The fire broke out at 6:00. At 6:15, the fire _____ sounded.
       afraid
       alarm

7. Many people came to the yard sale. _____ people came to the sale.
       numerous
       famous

8. The teacher did not like the way Jan acted in class. The teacher did not like how Jan _____ in class.
       belonged
       behaved

☐ Correct   ☐ Checking Up

LESSON 31

■ **New Sound.** Say the words.

sh<u>oo</u>k   b<u>oo</u>k

A. **New Words.** Say each sound. Say each word.

1. b<u>oo</u>k   sh<u>oo</u>k
2. bl<u>oo</u>m   c<u>oo</u>k
3. st<u>oo</u>d   sp<u>oo</u>l
4. f<u>oo</u>l   f<u>oo</u>t

5. The excited speaker shook his fist at the crowd.
6. We will cook the peas and corn in the steamer.
7. Mark stood in the rain until the bus arrived.
8. Which foot belongs on the gas pedal?

B. **Challenge Words.** Say the words.

woodpile   football   scooter   wooden   teaspoon
  1   2   1   2   1   2   1   2   1   2

moonlight fishhook   mushroom bookkeeper footlocker
  1   2   1   2   1   2   1   2   3   1   2   3

C. **Word Parts.** Say the word.

pass<u>ive</u>

D. **Words with Word Parts.** Say the words.

1. <u>a</u>dult   <u>re</u>sale   <u>pre</u>date   <u>con</u>cept
2. neg<u>ative</u>   shame<u>ful</u>   punish<u>able</u>   attract<u>ive</u>
3. <u>com</u>pliment   <u>re</u>gretful   expert<u>ness</u>   <u>in</u>cent<u>ive</u>
4. <u>re</u>tire<u>ment</u> complic<u>ation</u> except<u>ion</u>al <u>in</u>suffer<u>able</u>

E. **Sight Words.** Say the words.

enough   learn   anything   thought   almost
only   don't   father   sure   does

F. Passages. Read each part of the story. Write the story part number under the picture that goes with each story part.

Cork from Portugal

Part 1

Norm was in the den looking at this father's books. His father was sitting nearby reading the newspaper. After a while, Norm came over and stood by his father's chair. "Dad," Norm said, "will you help me think of a topic for my report? I want to write about something unusual, but I can't think of anything."

His father thought quietly for several moments, and then he said, "How about writing a report on mushrooms or lighthouses or cork? Cork might be your best choice. Not only is it an unusual topic, but your Uncle Gregg can tell you all about it. He worked on a cork farm in Portugal, you know. Why don't you give him a call?"

Part 2

The next day after school, Norm went to visit his uncle. They talked for a while, and then Norm said, "Uncle Gregg, I thought you were a retired bookkeeper. Dad said that you worked on a cork farm in Portugal. Can you tell me enough about cork so that I can write a report on it?"

"I am sure I can," Uncle Gregg said. "I worked on a cork farm most of my adult life. I only worked as a bookkeeper here because there are no cork farms in this part of the country. At times I still miss it. Well, sit there on that footstool and I will tell you all about cork."

Part 3

Uncle Gregg started by saying, "Most cork comes from the forests of Portugal. Cork comes from one kind of oak tree. It takes a lot of training for a cork stripper to learn how to strip cork from a tree without hurting the tree.

The first thing a cork stripper does is make two cuts in the tree bark. One is around the top of the tree trunk and the other is at the bottom of the trunk. Then the stripper makes a slice from the top to the bottom of the trunk. If the cork stripper has been careful, the cork will now peel off the tree, just like taking off the skin of a banana."

Uncle Gregg stopped at this point and said, "Why don't we eat dinner. Then I will continue to tell you about cork."

G. **Practice Activity 1.** Read each question. Look back at the story on page 125. Fill in each blank with the best word.

Part 1

1. What did Norm want his dad to do?

   He wanted his dad to help him think of a _____ for his _____.

2. What did Norm want to write about?

   He wanted to write about something _____.

3. Why did Norm's father suggest that Norm should call his uncle?

   Norm's father suggested that Norm should call Uncle _____ because he knows a lot about _____.

Part 2

4. Where did Norm go after school?

   Norm went to visit his _____.

5. Where had Uncle Gregg worked during most of his adult life?

   He had worked on a _____ _____.

Part 3

6. Where does most cork come from?

   Most cork comes from the _____ of _____.

7. What is the first thing that a cork stripper does?

   The first thing that a cork stripper does is to make _____ cuts in the _____ _____.

8. What does the cork stripper do next?

   The cork stripper makes a slice from the _____ down to the _____ of the trunk.

☐ Correct

H. Practice Activity 2. Read each list. Cross out the word that does not belong in each list.

1. woodpile
   sausage
   cabbage
   mushrooms

2. sunflower
   teaspoons
   sagebrush
   grapevines

3. penthouse
   playhouse
   stagecoach
   doghouse

4. bookkeeper
   snowplow
   widower
   homeowner

5. rowboat
   boathouse
   sailboat
   motorboat

6. scooter
   snowplow
   rowboat
   cowhide

7. football
   teaspoon
   basketball
   soccer

8. nightgown
   jacket
   trousers
   wooden

9. blowtorch
   crowbar
   mushroom
   hammer

☐ Correct

I. Practice Activity 3. Fill in each blank with the better word.

1. If you are a grown-up, you are an _____.
   adopt
   adult

2. If you stop something from happening, you _____ it.
   prepay
   prevent

3. If you did something that was wrong, it might be a _____ shameful thing to do.
   shameful
   cheerful

4. If you like someone very much, you might think that person is _____.
   attractive
   passive

5. If you went to the last track meet of the season, you would be at the _____ track meet.
   final
   mental

6. If something is very hard for you to do, you might have to _____ to finish it.
   gentle
   struggle

7. If you did something very fast, you would do it _____.
   swiftly
   nightly

8. If you don't stop working on something, you _____ working on it.
   concept
   continue

☐ Correct

127

LESSON 32

A. **New Words.** Say each sound. Say each word.

1. h<u>oo</u>d   sp<u>oo</u>l
2. h<u>oo</u>k   cr<u>oo</u>k
3. gl<u>oo</u>m   g<u>oo</u>d
4. br<u>oo</u>k   b<u>oo</u>st
5. The hood of my pink raincoat is torn.
6. You can find your coat on the hook to the right of the door.
7. *Where the Red Fern Grows* is a good book.
8. Watch the deer leap over the brook.

B. **Challenge Words.** Say the words.

cook·book   ball·room   foot·print   foot·rest   wood·craft
 1   2   1   2   1   2   1   2   1   2

rac·coon   car·toon   sham·poo   un·der·stood   wood·cut·ter
 1   2   1   2   1   2   1 2 3   1 2 3

C. **Word Parts.** Say the word.

pass<u>ive</u>

D. **Words with Word Parts.** Say the words.

1. <u>in</u>law   <u>dis</u>grace   <u>ex</u>ceed   <u>pre</u>side
2. aggress<u>ive</u>   marvel<u>ous</u>   form<u>al</u>   obtain<u>able</u>
3. <u>a</u>maze<u>ment</u>   <u>ex</u>clama<u>tion</u>   <u>in</u>act<u>ive</u>   <u>con</u>ceal<u>ment</u>
4. <u>ex</u>cep<u>tion</u>   <u>con</u>tent<u>ment</u>   <u>de</u>tach<u>ment</u>   <u>pre</u>concep<u>tion</u>

E. **Sight Words.** Say the words.

learn   enough   among   minute   live

year   also   almost   sure   told

F. Passages. Read each part of the story. Write the story part number under the picture that goes with each story part.

Norm Learns More

Part 1

    After dinner, Norm and Uncle Gregg returned to the den. Uncle Gregg placed some wood in the fireplace and started a fire. "That feels good," Norm said as he stood by the fire. "Will you tell me more about the cork farm now, Uncle Gregg?" he asked.

    They sat down, and Norm's uncle began to talk. "Well, I told you that cork strippers must be careful. If they cut too much cork or cut into the tree too deeply, they can hurt the tree. Cork will never grow again in the spot where the tree has been hurt.

    After the cork comes off the tree, the trunk of the tree turns a deep rust red. This is because tannin, a kind of powder in the tree trunk, turns red when air hits it. Tannin has many uses, but we can save that until your next report," Uncle Gregg said.

Part 2

    Uncle Gregg also explained that Portugal sells most of its cork. "Since cork is so important, there are rules to protect cork trees. One good rule is that a cork tree must be fifteen to twenty years old before it is first stripped. A tree that has been stripped of cork should not be stripped again until nine years have passed. Rules like these help keep the trees in good shape. Trees that are well cared for live three hundred to four hundred years."

    Uncle Gregg got up from his chair and went to stir the fire in the fireplace.

Part 3

    "Cork is marvelous," Uncle Gregg said. "It is very light because it is ninety-two percent air. It is not affected by heat, cold, liquids, or gas. It is also soundproof. Among other things, cork is used to make bottle stoppers and place mats." Then Uncle Gregg paused for a minute and said, "Well, Norm, I think I have told you all I know about cork. Do you think you have learned enough to write a report?" he asked.

    "I sure do, Uncle Gregg," Norm said. "Thank you for taking the time to explain all of this to me. My report is sure to be the most unusual one in my class."

G. **Practice Activity 1.** Read each question. Look back at the story on page 129. Fill in each blank with the best word.

Part 1

1. How can cork strippers hurt a tree?

   They can cut too much _____ or cut into the tree too _____.

2. How does the tree trunk change after the cork comes off?

   The trunk turns a deep _____ _____.

3. What is the powder in the tree trunk called?

   The powder is called _____.

Part 2

4. How old must a cork tree be before it is stripped?

   The cork tree must be _____ to _____ years old.

5. How many years must pass before a cork tree should be stripped again?

   At least _____ years must pass before a cork tree can be stripped again.

6. How many years can a cork tree live?

   A cork tree that is well cared for can live _____ _____ to _____ _____ years.

Part 3

7. What percent of cork is air?

   _____-_____ percent of cork is air.

8. What is cork used to make?

   Cork is used to make bottle _____ and _____ mats, among other things.

☐ Correct

H. **Practice Activity 2.** Read each story. Underline the endings that make sense.

1. Janis grows flowers in her garden. In the summer, Janis _____.
   a. shakes the snow off her plants
   b. looks at flowers blooming in the garden
   c. cuts the flowers off the plants

2. The winters in New York can be very cold. During one cold winter, Troy _____.
   a. put on a wool hood
   b. picked blooming flowers in the woods
   c. added wood to the fireplace

3. One afternoon, Gale went to the drugstore. At the drugstore, she got _____.
   a. a brook filled with water
   b. a book and a little wooden box
   c. a good book and a box of needles

4. One summer day, Maria went to the woods with her dog. In the woods, she _____.
   a. sat next to a brook
   b. stood on a footstool
   c. looked at the blooming flowers

☐ Correct

I. **Practice Activity 3.** Read each question. Underline the best words for each question.

1. Which words name animals?
   footprint   giraffe
   rabbit   raccoon
   woodcraft   woodchuck

2. Which words name people?
   woodcutter bookkeeper
   moonlight   footlocker
   townspeople cowhand

3. Which words name things you can get at a drugstore?
   understood toothbrush
   toothpaste shampoo
   woodpile   footprint

4. Which words name things you can ride in or on?
   seaplane   widower
   rowboat   scooter
   sailboat   stagecoach

5. Which words name rooms?
   bedroom   fishhook
   ballroom   woodcraft
   kitchen   bathroom

6. Which words name tools?
   blowtorch   hammer
   screwdriver footrest
   wrench   crowbar

7. Which words name things you can find in a kitchen?
   ballroom   teaspoon
   scooter   faucet
   cookbook   penthouse

8. Which words name sports?
   football   sunflower
   woodpile   baseball
   soccer   nightgown

☐ Correct

LESSON 33

A. New Words. Say each sound. Say each word.

1. h<u>oo</u>k   h<u>oo</u>p
2. w<u>oo</u>l   br<u>oo</u>k
3. bl<u>oo</u>m   w<u>oo</u>d
4. t<u>oo</u>k   tr<u>oo</u>ps
5. My coat was caught on this hook.
6. The wool curtains will keep out the cold wind.
7. Put the wood by the fireplace, please.
8. The train trip to the seacoast took five days.

B. Challenge Words. Say the words.

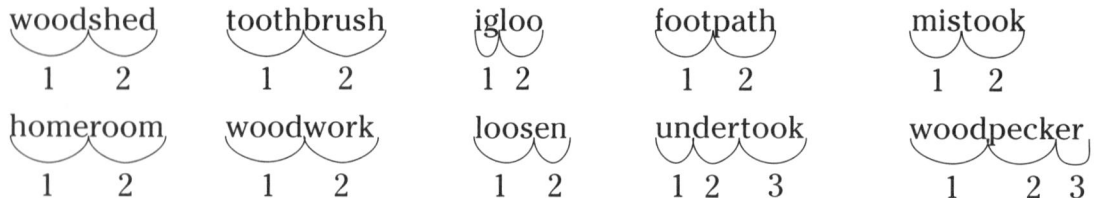

woodshed	toothbrush	igloo	footpath	mistook
1 2	1 2	1 2	1 2	1 2
homeroom	woodwork	loosen	undertook	woodpecker
1 2	1 2	1 2	1 2 3	1 2 3

C. Word Parts. Say the word.

pass<u>ive</u>

D. Words with Word Parts. Say the words.

1. <u>c</u>ommute   <u>a</u>buse   <u>re</u>frain   <u>ex</u>pel
2. offens<u>ive</u>   fat<u>al</u>   flaw<u>less</u>   obsess<u>ive</u>
3. <u>dis</u>creetly   <u>c</u>onstruct<u>ive</u>   norm<u>al</u>ly   <u>in</u>tersec<u>tion</u>
4. <u>de</u>tach<u>able</u>   <u>re</u>sent<u>ment</u>   <u>dis</u>respect<u>ful</u>   <u>ex</u>clus<u>ive</u>

E. Sight Words. Say the words.

| minute | among | enough | learn | only |
| their | thought | told | your | also |

F. **Passages.** Read each part of the story. Write the story part number under the picture that goes with each story part.

Dad and the Scouts

Part 1

Dad drove the car into the driveway and said to Mike, "When you get out, don't forget to take your sleeping bag and knapsack into the house. Tell Mom I will be there in a few minutes." Mike took his things and went in while Dad put the car away. When Dad went in, Mike was telling his mother all about their weekend camping trip.

Mom glanced at Dad, who looked exhausted. "Dinner will be in about an hour," she said. "Why don't you rest a little? I can get all the details from Mike," she said, trying to hide a smile.

"I think I could sleep for a week," Dad agreed as he sat down on the couch. "Call me if you need any help."

Part 2

Later, at the dinner table, Mike continued to tell his mother about the things he and the other boys in the scout troop had discovered in the woods. "We got to brush our teeth in the brook, and we even saw a woodpecker," Mike told his mother. "We also went for a long hike on the footpath around the lake. At night, we cooked hot dogs and beans over a campfire. It was tremendous!" Mike exclaimed.

They finished eating, and Mike said, "All the scouts said to thank you, Dad. They said you were a good sport too. I hope we can go back next year. Can we?"

"Let's wait and see, Mike," his dad said.

Part 3

After Mike was in bed, Mom said to Dad, "You look terrible! I thought you told Mike you were an expert Eagle Scout when you were a boy. What happened to you?"

"Don't make me remember it all," Dad groaned. "To start with, no one told me the tents had detachable flaps. I was the only scout leader who had to have a *kid* help him put up his tent! The next day we went on a hike. I thought hikes were *short* trips. My feet hurt so badly by the time we returned, I was ready to turn in all my Eagle Scout badges. Then we discovered a fatal mistake. My tent must have been pitched right on top of an anthill. The ant attack was in full swing by the time we got to my tent." Dad looked at Mom who was grinning widely. "It's not that funny. Did I tell you about the woodpecker that kept me awake all night with its pecking?"

G. **Practice Activity 1.** Read each question. Look back at the story on page 133. Fill in each blank with the best word.

Part 1

1. What did Dad and Mike do one weekend?

   They went on a _____ _____.

2. What did Mike take into the house?

   Mike took his _____ bag and his _____.

3. Who looked exhausted after the camping trip?

   _____ looked exhausted after the camping trip.

Part 2

4. Where had the scouts hiked?

   The scouts had hiked on a footpath around the _____.

5. What did the scouts do at night?

   At night, they cooked _____ _____ and _____ over a campfire.

6. What did the scouts say about Mike's father?

   They said that his father was a good _____.

Part 3

7. Why did Dad have ants in his tent?

   His tent was right on top of an _____.

8. Why didn't Dad get any sleep on the camping trip?

   A _____ kept Dad awake all night with his pecking.

☐ Correct

134

H. **Practice Activity 2.** Fill in each blank with the best word.

wool   hook   brook   hood
wood   took   shook   good

1. The baby _____ her rattle.
2. Martha _____ the children on a trip to the woods.
3. The _____ of the car was hot after the drive.
4. Because of the cold wind, Gene put on a _____ coat.
5. Would you rate this show as _____ or bad?
6. The flowers grew along the little _____.
7. Ted hung the plow blade on a large _____.
8. The footstool was made of _____.

☐ Correct

I. **Practice Activity 3.** Fill in each blank with the better word.

1. _____ people who work at the same factory _____ to work in one car.   commute / several
2. Because of Carla's _____ acts in class, the principal had to _____ Carla.   expel / terrible
3. The store got the _____ _____ of shirts just one day before the sale.   final / shipment
4. Every day Janis goes to an _____ class. She feels _____ after the class.   marvelous / exercise
5. Mark plans to continue his _____ at a trade school for _____.   adults / education
6. I was very _____ when I heard the fire _____ ring in the classroom.   alarm / afraid
7. This fall Kay plans to _____ the number of _____ in her herd to twenty.   cattle / increase

☐ Correct   ☐ Checking Up

135

LESSON 34

■ **New Sound.** Say the words.

dr<u>ea</u>d   m<u>ea</u>nt

A. **New Words.** Say each sound. Say each word.

1. thr<u>ea</u>d   d<u>ea</u>th
2. st<u>ea</u>l   m<u>ea</u>nt
3. spr<u>ea</u>d   m<u>ea</u>l
4. dr<u>ea</u>m   scr<u>ea</u>m
5. Please use green thread when you sew my socks.
6. I meant to say, "Turn right at the light."
7. Mick will spread the food out over the picnic table.
8. My dream job is to be a writer.

B. **Challenge Words.** Say the words.

weather (1 2)   peanut (1 2)   sunbeam (1 2)   headlight (1 2)   heavy (1 2)

homestead (1 2)   mealtime (1 2)   widespread (1 2)   seaweed (1 2)   leadership (1 2 3)

C. **Words with Word Parts.** Say the words.

1. <u>d</u>evise   <u>c</u>ompete   <u>p</u>rotest   <u>c</u>onfirm
2. adjust<u>able</u>   <u>d</u>ental   favor<u>able</u>   impress<u>ive</u>
3. <u>ex</u>tens<u>ive</u>   <u>a</u>mend<u>ment</u>   <u>d</u>efens<u>ive</u>   <u>c</u>onven<u>tion</u>
4. collect<u>ive</u><u>ly</u>   i<u>nn</u>ova<u>tion</u>   mean<u>ing</u><u>ful</u>   <u>in</u>termi<u>ss</u><u>ion</u>

D. **Sight Words.** Say the words.

heard   minute   enough   learn   thought

friends   almost   does   anything   don't

E. **Passages.** Read each part of the story. Write the story part number under the picture that goes with each story part.

Death Scream

Part 1

Marty, Rick, Kate, and Pat were all sitting in the dining room at Pat's house. Three of them were trying to convince Pat to come to the show with them. "You will have a good time without me," she said. "*Death Scream* does not sound like anything I would enjoy. Besides, the last time you dragged me to a show like that, I had bad dreams all night. I am surprised you are going to see it, Kate," Pat said meaningfully.

"I told them that if it was too terrible to watch, I would get up and leave," Kate said. "I heard that some parts of the film are impressive. I wish you would change your mind, Pat."

"Not a chance," Pat said, shaking her head.

Part 2

They continued discussing the film for a while. Finally, Kate, Rick, and Marty decided that Pat was definitely not going with them. Since it was close to showtime, they decided to leave. "I hope you all enjoy the show," Pat said sincerely as they left. "Let me know how you like it," she said to Kate.

After her friends left, Pat spoke to her mother. Pat explained why she had chosen not to go. "At one time, a film meant entertainment. I don't find it entertaining to be frightened out of my wits. I prefer to stay home. I hope Kate does not regret going to see it."

Part 3

The next day, Pat saw Kate at school. "Well, how was it?" Pat asked.

"I hate to admit it, but it was dreadful. I was afraid the whole time. I think I screamed six times. I was going to leave, but Rick and Marty teased me so much that I stayed. Besides, I think I might have been more afraid to walk home alone than to stay there. I would not tell the boys that, though. I sure learned my lesson! Next time I will stay home, too."

"I bet Rick and Marty were afraid, too," Pat said. "They will just refuse to admit it. I wish there was a way we could find out what they really thought about it." Pat grinned. "Let's ask around, shall we?"

F. **Practice Activity 1.** Read each question. Look back at the story on page 137. Fill in each blank with the best word.

Part 1

1. What did Marty, Rick, and Kate want Pat to do?

   They wanted Pat to come to the _____ with them.

2. What was the name of the show?

   The name of the show was _____ _____.

3. Why didn't Pat want to go to the show?

   She had bad _____ after the last time she went to a show like *Death Scream*.

Part 2

4. Who went to the show?

   _____, _____, and _____ went to the show.

5. Whom did Pat speak with when her friends left?

   Pat spoke with her _____.

Part 3

6. What did Kate say about the show?

   Kate said that the show was _____.

7. How did Kate feel during the show?

   She was _____ the whole time.

8. Why didn't Kate leave when she became afraid?

   Rick and Marty _____ her so much that she stayed.

☐ Correct

G. Practice Activity 2. Read each list. Cross out the word that does not belong in each list.

1. lightning
   weather
   leadership
   thunder

2. seaweed
   sagebrush
   pencil
   bamboo

3. sunbeam
   moonlight
   seaweed
   flashlight

4. woodpecker
   giraffe
   gopher
   widespread

5. breakfast
   mealtime
   heavy
   dinner

6. peanut
   mushroom
   marshmallow
   homestead

7. homeroom
   headlight
   classmates
   classroom

8. football
   basketball
   headlight
   soccer

9. nightgown
   weather
   trousers
   jacket

☐ Correct

H. Practice Activity 2. Fill in each blank with the better word.

1. If you played a trumpet in a contest, you would _____ in the contest.   complete / compete

2. If you went to a dentist, you would have some _____ work done on your teeth.   dental / final

3. If you really liked something or were very impressed by something, it would be _____.   impressive / negative

4. If you had a belt that could adjust to many sizes, the belt would be _____.   adjustable / portable

5. If you really liked someone's plan and were in favor of it, the plan would be _____ to you.   punishable / favorable

6. If you work out a plan to do something, you _____ a plan.   devise / decrease

7. If you take a train to and from work every day, you _____ by train.   commute / combine

8. If you had a number of plants in your greenhouse, you would have _____ plants.   formal / several

☐ Correct

LESSON 35

A. **New Words.** Say each sound. Say each word.

1. h<u>ea</u>vy   t<u>ea</u>ch
2. wh<u>ea</u>t   dr<u>ea</u>d
3. h<u>ea</u>ther   ch<u>ea</u>p
4. b<u>ea</u>ch   d<u>ea</u>lt
5. I ate a heavy breakfast this morning.
6. What do you dread the most about airplane rides?
7. The purple heather grows on the hillside.
8. I dealt you some cards while you fixed our snacks.

B. **Challenge Words.** Say the words.

increase	leather	instead	meantime	pleasant
1 2	1 2	1 2	1 2	1 2
weapon	feather	cream puff	meadow	teacher
1 2	1 2	1 2	1 2	1 2

C. **Words with Word Parts.** Say the words.

1. <u>in</u>dex   <u>a</u>blaze   <u>di</u>stress   <u>pro</u>voke
2. tentat<u>ive</u>   dread<u>ful</u>   pardon<u>able</u>   effect<u>ive</u>
3. <u>com</u>prehens<u>ive</u>   <u>re</u>flect<u>ive</u>   <u>ex</u>haustion   <u>ex</u>pert<u>ness</u>
4. <u>com</u>mand<u>ment</u>   <u>a</u>bras<u>ive</u>   <u>ac</u>compl<u>ish</u>   <u>in</u>vent<u>iveness</u>

D. **Sight Words.** Say the words.

| heard | though | minute | among | enough |
| friend | thought | another | any | over |

E. Passages. Read each part of the story. Write the story part number under the picture that goes with each story part.

A Flawless Plan

Part 1

For several days after she saw *Death Scream*, Kate continued to talk to Pat about it. "Did I tell you that the night I saw it, I had a difficult time falling asleep? The next morning, my bedspread was all bunched up on the bed. I must have had bad dreams all night. What a mistake that was! I wish I had stayed home instead. Have you heard anything about what Rick and Marty thought of it?" Kate asked her friend.

"They claim it was a *mild* film and there was nothing to account for all your distress," Pat said. "I have another thought, though. Come over after school, and I will tell you about it."

Part 2

After school, Pat and Kate sat on lawn chairs in the backyard, and Pat disclosed her plan. "I have a feeling those boys were afraid, too. They are simply trying to provoke you with all that talk about a 'mild' film. I think it's a cheap trick, so this is what we are going to do. First, we need to make a deal with my little brother."

Kate looked puzzled. Pat said, "I heard the boys are having a meeting in their clubhouse Thursday afternoon. All we need to do is to have Brad plant a tape recorder inside the clubhouse. Then he will get Rick and Marty to talk about *Death Scream*. We will get all their comments on tape."

Part 3

Thursday afternoon, Pat and Kate were waiting for Brad to put the tape recorder inside the clubhouse. Kate asked Pat, "Did you have any problems with Brad? Does he know what to do?"

"He knows what to do, the little crook! I have to clean his room for a week for this. When Marty and Rick are in the clubhouse, Brad will bring them a bowl of popcorn. Then Brad will ask them about the film and leave. I hope it works!"

Two hours later, the boys' meeting was over. Brad gave the tape recorder to his sister and left with a pleasant smile. The girls checked different parts of the tape until they heard Marty say, "We cannot let Kate or Pat find out. At one point, I thought I was going to be sick. . . . I wanted Kate to leave so I could go, too. . . ." Pat and Kate grinned when they heard this.

F. **Practice Activity 1.** Read each question. Look back at the story on page 141. Fill in each blank with the best word.

Part 1

1. What happened to Kate after she saw *Death Scream*?

    She had bad _____ all night.

2. What did Kate wish she had done instead of going to the show?

    She wished that she had stayed _____ instead of going to the show.

3. What did the boys say about the film?

    They said the film was very _____.

Part 2

4. How did Pat think the boys felt about the show?

    Pat thought the boys were _____, too.

5. What did Brad put inside the boys' clubhouse?

    He put a _____ _____ inside the boys' clubhouse.

6. What did the girls want the boys to talk about?

    They wanted the boys to talk about the film _____ _____.

Part 3

7. What did the girls do with the tape recorder?

    They checked _____ parts of the _____.

8. What did the girls hear Marty say about the film?

    The girls heard Marty say that he thought he was going to be _____ during the show.

☐ Correct

G. Practice Activity 2. Read each question. Underline the best words for each question.

1. Which words name people?
   teacher   widow
   cowhand   pleasant
   bookkeeper   homeowner

2. Which words name places?
   leather   bedspread
   meadow   feather
   homeroom   footpath

3. Which words name things?
   feather   teacher
   woodpecker   leather
   toothbrush   headlight

4. Which words name plants?
   sagebrush   woodpecker
   sunflowers   cabbage
   pine tree   cream puff

5. Which words tell about meals?
   mealtime   breakfast
   lunch   weapon
   picnic   dinner

6. Which words name things you can eat?
   peanut   marshmallow
   leather   toothbrush
   cream puff   chowder

7. Which words tell how you may feel?
   pleasant   woodshed
   unhappy   mealtime
   happy   terrific

8. Which words tell about weather?
   lightning   headlights
   outgrown   thunder
   sunshine   peanuts

☐ Correct

H. Practice Activity 3. Fill in each blank with the better word.

1. The _____ of shells did not have a flaw.   flawless
   The collection was _____.   collection

2. Your lateness is _____ if you have an   excuse
   _____.   pardonable

3. Seat belts need to be _____. To operate   adjustable
   _____, seat belts need to be tight.   safely

4. A _____ was placed on the lawn in front   monument
   of the school. It is a monument to good _____.   education

5. When Janis went to _____ in the speech contest,   speechless
   she was _____.   compete

6. Every day Ms. Archer _____ to work on an   commutes
   _____ subway train. This subway train stops   express
   only twice.

☐ Correct

LESSON 36

A. **New Words.** Say each sound. Say each word.

1. d<u>ea</u>f   h<u>ea</u>p
2. f<u>ea</u>st   w<u>ea</u>ther
3. h<u>ea</u>lth   p<u>ea</u>ch
4. bl<u>ea</u>ch   spr<u>ea</u>d
5. Some fish in the deep sea are deaf.
6. Watch the weather report on the news.
7. My health club has a large swimming pool.
8. Sam likes to spread jam on his toast.

B. **Challenge Words.** Say the words.

pheasant	seasick	sweater	preacher	headdress
1 2	1 2	1 2	1 2	1 2
seacoast	spreader	leaflet	gingerbread	letterhead
1 2	1 2	1 2	1 2 3	1 2 3

C. **Words with Word Parts.** Say the words.

1. <u>pro</u>ceed   <u>a</u>live   <u>pre</u>cise   <u>ex</u>cel
2. <u>per</u>cept<u>ive</u>   <u>pro</u>sper<u>ous</u>   peace<u>able</u>   need<u>less</u>
3. <u>pro</u>gress<u>ive</u>   <u>de</u>struct<u>ive</u>   <u>pre</u>dic<u>tion</u>   <u>a</u>bol<u>ish</u>
4. <u>com</u>plain<u>ing</u>   <u>pre</u>vent<u>ive</u>   <u>un</u>skill<u>ful</u><u>ly</u>   <u>a</u>stonish<u>ing</u><u>ly</u>

D. **Sight Words.** Say the words.

though	enough	through	throughout	among
again	don't	year	thought	almost

E. **Passages.** Read each part of the story. Write the story part number under the picture that goes with each story part.

The Last Picnic

Part 1

Stan and Eve were in the kitchen packing the picnic basket. "I am glad the weather is so nice," Eve said. "This is likely to be our last picnic this summer. The summer sure went quickly, don't you think?"

"I agree," Stan said. "That's one reason I want to make this a real feast. So far I have hot dogs and hamburgers, peaches, tea, and gingerbread cake. What other things do we need?" asked Stan.

"We should take a blanket to sit on, and maybe we should take sweaters. The seacoast gets cool at night. Barb and Jack will arrive soon. It's close to noon, and they are both astonishingly precise."

Part 2

Shortly after noon, they packed the car and headed for Lighthouse Bay. "I hope you have heaps of food in that basket," Jack said. "By the time we get there, I will be ready to eat."

"That's not news, Jack. I have known you to eat throughout the entire day," Eve said. "It beats me how you stay so disgustingly thin."

"All that food keeps me in good health," Jack said with a grin. "My mother says I am still a growing boy. Besides, don't forget that I run seven miles a day!" A short time later they reached Lighthouse Bay and parked the car close to the beach.

Part 3

"Stan, spread the blanket by the rocks," called Barb. "I will set the food out, and we can snack until the fire gets going."

"Eve and I will go find some bleached driftwood for the bonfire," Jack said. "Make sure there is enough for us to eat when we get back. On second thought, maybe you should get the driftwood, and we should spread out the food!"

They spent a pleasant afternoon playing ball, snacking, and swimming. Around six they started the fire and roasted hot dogs and hamburgers. When it got dark, they carefully doused the fire and got ready to leave. All agreed that the last picnic of the summer had been the best one.

F. **Practice Activity 1.** Read each question. Look back at the story on page 145. Fill in each blank with the best word.

Part 1

1. Why did Stan want to make the picnic a real feast?

   It was the _____ picnic of the summer.

2. What did Stan pack for the picnic?

   He packed hot _____, hamburgers, peaches, tea, and gingerbread _____.

3. Why did Eve think that they should take sweaters?

   She thought they should take sweaters because the seacoast gets

   _____ at _____.

Part 2

4. Where did they go for their picnic?

   They went to _____ _____.

5. What did Jack hope they had in the basket?

   He hoped that they had heaps of _____ in the basket.

6. Why does Jack stay so thin?

   One reason is that Jack runs _____ _____ a day.

Part 3

7. How did they spend the afternoon?

   They played _____, snacked, and went _____.

8. What did they all agree on at the end of the picnic?

   They all agreed that the last picnic of the summer had been the

   _____ one.

☐ Correct

G. **Practice Activity 2.** Read each story. Underline the endings that make sense.

1. One Saturday, Kay went to the store to get food for lunch. At the store, she got _____.
   a. a loaf of wheat bread
   b. cheese spread and crackers
   c. toothpaste and shampoo

2. Ms. Floyd likes to get things on sale. One day, Ms. Floyd got _____.
   a. two boxes of thread that were half-price
   b. a very thick steak for a high price
   c. six loaves of French bread for a very cheap price

3. Mark really likes to play checkers. On Thursday night, he _____.
   a. put the checkerboard on the table
   b. cooked steaks on a grill
   c. placed the checkers on the board

4. Barb takes very good care of her things. One morning, Barb _____.
   a. used a needle and thread to mend her bedspread
   b. placed her lace bedspread in a large box
   c. broke all of her heavy dishes

☐ Correct

H. **Practice Activity 3.** Fill in each blank with the better word.

1. If something has a heartbeat, it is _____.
   alive / abuse

2. If you are very good at a subject in school, you _____ in that subject.
   excel / excuse

3. If you had lots of wealth, you would be _____.
   numerous / prosperous

4. If you did something that did not need to be done, what you did was _____.
   needless / endless

5. If you went ahead and did something, you would _____.
   proceed / protest

6. If a house was on fire, the house would be _____.
   ablaze / alive

7. If a jewel did not have one flaw, it would be _____.
   nameless / flawless

8. If you have work done on your teeth, you would have _____ work done.
   normal / dental

☐ Correct   ☐ Checking Up

147

Word Lists

LESSON 1	LESSON 2	LESSON 3	LESSON 4	LESSON 5	LESSON 6	LESSON 7	LESSON 8
New Words	**New Words**	**New Words**	**New Words**	**New Words**	**New Words**	**New Words**	**New Words**
food	moon	room	yawn	fraud	law	boil	join
soon	cool	loose	fault	straw	choose	boy	jail
feed	show	stool	claw	stool	pause	point	toy
flirt	noon	root	haul	dream	lawn	paint	tea
broom	sheet	steal	float	drawn	thaw	Roy	spoil
flow	tool	roof	draw	vault	sprawl	pawn	toil
spoon	shoot	booth	spool	hawk	sprain	joy	maul
brain	moose	mood	crawl	freed	jaw	soil	Floyd
smooth	boast	beach	cool	shawl	jar	goose	spool
choose	boost	hoop	lawn	flow	paw	coin	moist
sport	moan	lease	loan	flaw	throw	cool	crawl
tooth	snooze	bloom	cause	flee	launch	noise	Troy
Challenge Words	**Challenge Words**	**Challenge Words**	**Challenge Words**	**Challenge Words**	**Challenge Words**	**Challenge Words**	**Challenge Words**
rooster	harpoon	dustproof	exhaust	applause	pauper	turmoil	soybean
scooter	moonbeam	booster	author	coleslaw	sawmill	employ	noiseless
moonlight	whirlpool	loosen	auburn	withdrawn	because	enjoy	annoy
cartoon	noontime	baboon	August	sawdust	seesaw	destroy	loiter
toothbrush	monsoon	tattoo	drawing	drawback	awesome	tinfoil	exploit
schoolroom	homeroom	foolproof	lawn mower	autumn	launder	boycott	toy shop
teaspoon	classroom	mushroom	lawyer	sweepstakes	autoharp	joyride	charcoal
shampoo	plaintiff	drainpipe	igloo	wayside	automatic	oyster	corduroy
raccoon	harbor	president	imperfect	bridegroom	misinterpret	appointment	employee
afternoon	increase	innkeeper	advertise	entertainment	understood	sharpshooter	employer
Sight Words	**Sight Words**	**Sight Words**	**Sight Words**	**Sight Words**	**Sight Words**	**Sight Words**	**Sight Words**
all	all	all	other	other	other	old	old
call	tall	fall	another	another	another	cold	fold
hall	ball	call	mother	brother	mother	told	cold
ball	fall	hall	brother	brother	brother	gold	told
tall	call	tall	many	many	many	sold	hold
because	because	about	also	also	through	one	give
through	also	because	call	animals	also	other	other
also	through	want	find	because	one	many	about
about	about	through	about	want	want	another	through
care	find	also	been	there	about	about	find
find	where	put	come	what	would	want	all
were	your	now	people	were	how	all	would
one	now	one	there	now	from	there	were
your	how	find	were	call	now	come	there
who	why	been				what	want
some							
how							
many							

LESSON 9	LESSON 10	LESSON 11	LESSON 12	LESSON 13	LESSON 14	LESSON 15
New Words	**New Words**	**New Words**	**New Words**	**New Words**	**New Words**	**New Words**
coil	new	chew	flew	out	our	sprout
coat	noise	paw	paws	joint	oil	coach
coy	grew	threw	blew	round	sound	couch
toy	grain	crew	new	shawl	cloud	sprawl
paints	chew	join	shrew	cloud	claw	trout
points	stew	blew	proof	loose	south	mouth
fail	news	grew	news	house	ground	haul
foil	fee	brew	stream	blew	mouse	grouch
pawn	dew	shown	drew	shout	scoot	spout
toil	drawn	joy	threw	proud	moist	ouch
tool	drew	crawl	strewn	blouse	scout	threw
poise	flew	shrew	joys	blown	hound	flour
Challenge Words	**Challenge Words**	**Challenge Words**	**Challenge Words**	**Challenge Words**	**Challenge Words**	**Challenge Words**
enjoy	jewel	sewer	newsstand	counter	without	outgrew
ointment	newsstand	cashew	Lewis	thousand	playground	dismount
poison	newscast	unscrew	sewer	surround	madhouse	farmhouse
convoy	chewable	mildew	dewdrop	countless	outside	account
broiler	New York	newborn	August	southwest	cloudless	countless
avoid	newspaper	newsreel	newsprint	doghouse	discount	Boy Scout
embroider	screwdriver	crewneck	frustrate	outburst	thundercloud	outlaw
disappoint	newsletter	seaplane	classmates	trousers	underground	scoutmaster
destroyer	subscribe	jeweler	proofread	outspoken	southwestern	outstanding
enjoyment	storekeeper	authorize	appointment	encounter	fellowship	counterclockwise
Sight Words	**Sight Words**	**Sight Words**	**Sight Words**	**Sight Words**	**Sight Words**	**Sight Words**
old	find	find	find	walk	walk	walk
cold	mind	mind	mind	talk	talk	talk
sold	kind	kind	kind	coming	warm	woman
fold	over	give	over	woman	woman	women
told	give	over	give	even	even	over
give	told	mother	told	now	over	even
many	about	one	other	kind	kind	warm
other	another	told	another	want	also	there
also	what	your	through	about	through	told
through	who	about	want	another	went	come
come	could	where	all	cold	mother	many
were	come	many	about	some	give	where
there	now	why	many			
work	good					
find						

LESSON 16	LESSON 17	LESSON 18	LESSON 19	LESSON 20	LESSON 21	LESSON 22	LESSON 23
New Words	**New Words**	**New Words**	**New Words**	**New Words**	**New Words**	**New Words**	**New Words**
knot	phone	know	dodge	ridge	hitch	cell	force
wreck	quest	phone	catch	pitch	bridge	glance	mice
quit	phase	wrench	edge	phone	switch	stick	cause
knight	quiz	quit	sketch	know	math	cone	cinch
phone	math	knife	judge	grudge	nudge	voice	place
knob	wring	wrung	snatch	quote	Mitch	twice	crow
graph	phrase	wrist	witch	fudge	ditch	clip	since
knife	quake	thick	chase	hatch	blotch	space	cape
wrote	quote	quick	patch	badge	budge	trick	fence
kneel	quite	knew	itch	match	scratch	peace	cease
quilt	write	sphinx	lodge	wedge	swish	came	crawl
wrap	knit	knelt	lock	path	latch	cent	price
Challenge Words	**Challenge Words**	**Challenge Words**	**Challenge Words**	**Challenge Words**	**Challenge Words**	**Challenge Words**	**Challenge Words**
dolphin	gopher	sulphur	catcher	hatchback	pitchfork	circus	cartwheel
wrapper	knapsack	playwright	hodgepodge	pitchfork	drawbridge	canteen	center
jackknife	quiver	unknown	pitcher	misjudge	stretcher	blockade	embrace
shipwreck	orphan	liquid	outstretch	phonics	hopscotch	cinder	cedar
knapsack	shipwreck	knuckle	hatchet	bamboo	switchover	absence	pencil
knothole	knockout	phantom	hitchhike	coastline	graphite	spacecraft	kneecap
vanquish	banquet	writer	patchwork	authentic	gopher	second	democrat
kneecap	wrinkle	tranquil	kitchen	autograph	yard line	electric	committee
underline	emphasis	squirrel	underneath				
handwritten	equipment	sophomore	referee				
Sight Words	**Sight Words**	**Sight Words**	**Sight Words**	**Sight Words**	**Sight Words**	**Sight Words**	**Sight Words**
don't	sure	sure	only	even	their	every	heard
even	don't	only	most	does	only	their	any
coming	care	again	does	most	most	does	every
find	even	hold	again	only	even	only	their
two	two	about	sure	again	does	sure	don't
sure	were	your	four	through	many	told	talk
work	should	also	also	their	also	find	about
about	about	give	many	many	find	your	some
told	put	want	some	also	some	talk	through
woman	others	would	walk	about	over	again	there
give			another				
machine			hour				

150

LESSON 24	LESSON 25	LESSON 26	LESSON 27	LESSON 28	LESSON 29	LESSON 30	LESSON 31
New Words	**New Words**	**New Words**	**New Words**	**New Words**	**New Words**	**New Words**	**New Words**
prance	cringe	germ	surge	owl	frown	flower	book
curb	cage	stage	goose	blown	brow	crow	shook
couch	gee	gem	gist	flown	growl	crown	bloom
cliff	gent	age	green	plow	slow	town	cook
cents	glee	glad	pages	clown	growth	grow	stood
prince	merge	urge	gash	show	bowl	powder	spool
choice	gust	large	bulge	down	shown	gown	fool
crew	page	goose	glee	crowd	brown	glow	foot
lace	strange	grew	range				
cool	change	drug	stage				
nice	gate	Gene	merge				
Rick	gist	sponge	ranger				
Challenge Words	**Challenge Words**	**Challenge Words**	**Challenge Words**	**Challenge Words**	**Challenge Words**	**Challenge Words**	**Challenge Words**
citrus	margin	ginger	drugstore	showtime	snowdrift	cowhide	woodpile
faucet	gently	disgust	danger	grown-up	downstream	rowboat	football
playwright	cabbage	target	gateway	owner	snowplow	nightgown	scooter
census	percent	sagebrush	carpool	chowder	homeowner	penthouse	wooden
boycott	teenage	greenhouse	giraffe	cowhand	blowtorch	outgrown	teaspoon
cloister	sausage	stagecoach	urgent	crowbar	fellowship	sunflower	moonlight
civil	German	Pacific	congress	sundown	gunpowder	widower	fishhook
countess	grapevine	gingersnap	autograph	somehow	townsman	marshmallow	mushroom
							bookkeeper
							footlocker
Sight Words	**Sight Words**	**Sight Words**	**Sight Words**	**Sight Words**	**Sight Words**	**Sight Words**	**Sight Words**
any	father	father	year	thought	thought	friend	enough
every	year	year	father	friend	someone	thought	learn
their	their	care	don't	anyway	friend	almost	anything
don't	every	women	give	someone	only	anyone	thought
only	again	any	does	somehow	any	every	almost
one	even	their	many	were	their	over	only
kind	two	talk	hold	sure	care	sure	don't
another	many	over	through	two	over	told	father
from	others	other	also	their	sure	another	sure
walk	through	also	mind	kind	don't	even	does

LESSON 32	LESSON 33	LESSON 34	LESSON 35	LESSON 36
New Words	**New Words**	**New Words**	**New Words**	**New Words**
hood	hook	thread	heavy	deaf
spool	hoop	death	teach	heap
hook	wool	steal	wheat	feast
crook	brook	meant	dread	weather
gloom	bloom	spread	heather	health
good	wood	meal	cheap	peach
brook	took	dream	beach	bleach
boost	troops	scream	dealt	spread
Challenge Words	**Challenge Words**	**Challenge Words**	**Challenge Words**	**Challenge Words**
cookbook	woodshed	weather	increase	pheasant
ballroom	toothbrush	peanut	leather	seasick
footprint	igloo	sunbeam	instead	sweater
footrest	footpath	headlight	meantime	preacher
woodcraft	mistook	heavy	pleasant	headdress
raccoon	homeroom	homestead	weapon	seacoast
cartoon	woodwork	mealtime	feather	spreader
shampoo	loosen	widespread	cream puff	leaflet
understood	undertook	seaweed	meadow	gingerbread
woodcutter	woodpecker	leadership	teacher	letterhead
Sight Words	**Sight Words**	**Sight Words**	**Sight Words**	**Sight Words**
learn	minute	heard	heard	though
enough	among	minute	though	enough
among	enough	enough	minute	through
minute	learn	learn	among	throughout
live	only	thought	enough	among
year	their	friends	friend	again
also	thought	almost	thought	don't
almost	told	does	another	year
sure	your	anything	any	thought
told	also	don't	over	almost